Inclusive Banking In India

Lalitagauri Kulkarni · Vasant Chintaman Joshi

Inclusive Banking In India

Re-imagining The Bank Business Model

palgrave
macmillan

Lalitagauri Kulkarni
Gokhale Institute of Politics and Economics
Mumbai, Maharashtra, India

Vasant Chintaman Joshi
Bank of India
Mumbai, Maharashtra, India

ISBN 978-981-33-6796-8 ISBN 978-981-33-6797-5 (eBook)
https://doi.org/10.1007/978-981-33-6797-5

This Palgrave Macmillan imprint is published by the registered company Springer Nature Singapore Pte Ltd.
The registered company address is: 152 Beach Road, #21-01/04 Gateway East, Singapore 189721, Singapore

To my parents
Mr. Rajendra Banhatti and Dr.Mrs. Vasundhara Banhatti

— Lalitagauri Kulkarni

To the bank personnel for continuing to serve the public
and keeping the flag flying during the worst of times…

—Vasant Chintaman Joshi & Lalitagauri Kulkarni

Preface

In the vast pool of literature on financial inclusion, there exist very few books dealing exclusively with this subject. This book proposes that the narrative of inclusive finance must change. Inclusive finance is not a privilege to be 'given to the poor'. It is their right to be included in the system. In India, the vast segment of population that is thus far unbanked and deprived is pigeon-holed at the bottom of the pyramid. We contend that this perception of describing the poor as the bottom of a hierarchical structure must change. The prevalent system of financial institutions should perceive them not as the *bottom of the pyramid* but as the *bulk of the population.*

The primary focus of the book is on how banks can cater to this silent majority. Banks need to make changes to their business model to use financial technology and undertake the work of microfinancing directly instead of outsourcing it. This idea is the central theme of our conceptual framework. Thus, the discussion is purposefully kept limited to inclusive banking implying bank account ownership and microlending, payments and money transfer, and does not extend to broader areas of financial inclusion like microinsurance.

The first chapter of the book discusses how inclusive finance has become indispensable in the present times when the volatility in the financial sector has turned into an abysmal fear of the future of the economies. Global pandemic has shown the world how the vulnerability and helplessness of the poor are a ticking time-bomb on which elitist systems stand.

If left unaddressed, this can turn the entire socio-economic and political system upside down. The chapter gives an overview of the concept and scope of inclusive banking, its evolution through various initiatives and the current policy stance on it.

A major portion of the literature on financial inclusion consists of empirical studies establishing the relation between inclusive finance and economic growth. Theorizing this relationship is essential as it helps to establish the general applicability and predictability of this nexus between inclusive finance and economic growth. Chapter 2 delves into the discussion of finance and financial inclusion in the framework of economic theory. It deliberates on the justification of banking for the poor from the perspectives of economic theory.

The ideological problem of whether banks should act as commercial profit maximizing institutions or should meet the needs of the society is discussed in Chapter 3. It provides an overview of the current trends in microlending by commercial banks and the issues and challenges faced by them in implementing the policy of financial inclusion to achieve the social goals.

Chapter 4 argues that the dependency of the non-bank microfinance sector, on the banks raises important questions. The fact that the NBFC microfinance is for profit, is not lending at the rates cheaper than the mainstream system and is vulnerable to shocks leads one to explore better alternative in the mainstream bank lending.

A bank may choose to enter the microfinance market directly, rather than through partnership with MFIs. For the success of inclusive finance, banks need to treat low-income segment as the core business rather than as an unwanted responsibility. Banks have a comparative advantage over the microfinance institutions. Shocks to the economy like COVID-19 pandemic prove that the microfinance institutions have limitations and the financial inclusion ecosystem cannot successfully and effectively achieve its goals without a more dynamic approach by banks.

Many studies confirm that escape from poverty through participation in microfinance is slow and uncertain. Chapter 5 delves into the political economy of inclusive finance. The political economy approach points out that the banking framework depends on the ideology of the state. Political pressures, lobbies and interest groups undermine the implementation of best practices. This has been experienced by the breach of lending practices and frauds in many countries including India.

Chapter 6 reviews the role of government schemes and reflects that the outcomes of financial inclusion initiatives are less than expected. The return on investment on all these initiatives has been negligible, taking into account the system costs. Many a time, the priority sector loans are given only to meet the targets. However, just an increase in the number of accounts and amounts of microloans does not make a difference in the lives of excluded persons. One cannot expect a poor individual to become an entrepreneur overnight and be successful in his microenterprise.

Chapter 7 discusses four evolving developments in the social and inclusive finance sector in India, viz. (i) digital revolution in inclusive finance sector, (ii) launching social stock exchange, (iii) microenterprise collaboratives and (iv) MFIs converted into banks and small finance banks. These developments may result in reducing costs and make inclusive banking viable. For instance, digital lending results in reduction in the cost of lending and consequently lending rates. Similarly, the development of social stock exchange can be expected to lessen the banks' burden of financing MFIs and NGOs and the banks can be free to independently forge into the microlending arena.

Chapter 8 presents a new business model for banks that proposes they should nurture the poor as their core client base. This should lead to a long-term relationship not restricted to borrowing. We postulate that the proposed business model would be financially viable with the newer avenues of cost reduction, digital lending, lean banking and advanced technology.

Finally, for successful inclusive banking, in addition to the accessible branch offices and convenient products, what is important is treating the customers with respect. Inclusion will be achieved only when the bank account operations are simple in local language and the bankers ensure that customers do not feel embarrassed by their lack of skills and education. From the bankers' viewpoint, they will be motivated to achieve this only when they stop thinking that these accounts are externally imposed. They need to be convinced that these accounts are viable and can be operated as regular accounts. The proposed model is an attempt to provide a roadmap for the inclusive banking policy in India.

Mumbai, India

Lalitagauri Kulkarni
Vasant Chintaman Joshi

Acknowledgements

We would like to express our gratitude to Prof. Abhijit Banerjee for his encouraging comments at the time of the release of this book at the convocation ceremony of Gokhale Institute of Politics and Economics. The present work is a culmination of our discussions with experts in the microfinance industry, interactions with bankers and field surveys of microlending institutions, self-help groups and entrepreneurial collaboratives throughout Maharashtra and southern parts of India. We thank Dr. Aloysius Fernandez, Dr. Madhura Chatrapathy, Dr. Medha Samant, Mr. G. Nagaraj and many others involved in microlending field for their valuable comments and support for the field surveys.

We are also grateful to the beneficiaries of the self-help groups, women's collaboratives and slum dwellers of Pune who gave us an opportunity to talk with them to have an idea of their perceptions, outlook and aspirations regarding their finances.

We are thankful to Prof. Rajas Parchure, RBI Chair Professor and Director of Gokhale Institute for the valuable comments on the development of the financial component of the new bank business model.

Gokhale Institute of Politics and Economics, Pune, provided us access to its library and infrastructure for the underlying study for this book.

We express our gratitude to the editors of Palgrave Macmillan Pvt. Ltd. and Springer Nature for standing by us throughout the process of finalizing the book. Without their support, the book would not have seen the light of day within the stipulated time frame.

All the while we counted upon the cheerful support of our family members.

Kirti, Achala and Sameer Deshpande actively contributed to the tedious task of formatting and editing the manuscript. Special thanks are due to Ranjit and Kimaya Kulkarni for their unconditional support and candid comments on the manuscript.

Contents

List of Figures

List of Tables

CHAPTER 1

Inclusive Banking—Concept and Context

Background

This book on inclusive banking is being published at a time when the age-old pandemic of poverty has been agonizingly intensified by the vagaries of the novel virus. In countries like India, this crisis has brought into focus the glaring gaps in governance and lack of resilience of the existing system to handle such shocks on a large scale. The UNCTAD Report (2020) projects that 120 million people will be pushed into extreme poverty in the developing world, with close to 300 million facing food insecurity. India with its dense population is caught between the pandemic and poverty. The report projected that the Indian economy will contract by 5.9% in 2020.

Behind the dry statistics are crores of informal sector workers grappling with the worry of feeding their families. The worst part is that the epidemic has crushed the aspirations of many in the informal sector at the margins who have lost their sundry jobs and other sources of earning. Their optimism is tainted and they are now questioning the prospect of ever coming out of the poverty!

Financial inclusion plays a crucial role during such challenging times. Microlending and insurance have a potential to safeguard the poor from being pushed to below the subsistence levels of living. The microfinance sector globally is facing financial problems because of disruptions in economic activities of the beneficiary members owing to the pandemic.

L. Kulkarni and V. C. Joshi, *Inclusive Banking In India*,
https://doi.org/10.1007/978-981-33-6797-5_1

Banks are an important link to transfer the governmental benefits to the poor. Governments and central banks are making all-out efforts to reduce the sufferings of those afflicted by the pandemic. Governments all over the world have announced fiscal stimulus in the form of cash benefit transfers to help vulnerable groups severely affected by the pandemic. In India, the direct benefit transfer schemes of the government have helped the poor through direct transfer of cash in their PM Jan Dhan Yojana (PMJDY) accounts. The government's stimulus revived many of the unused idle PMJDY accounts in India. The crisis underlined the importance of banking access and those who never operated a bank account also realized its importance. The direct benefit transfers during the crisis times made the marginalized, unbanked people aware of the need of participating in the formal system by opening a bank account. However, banks do not have any special scheme or model for these times. As the banks did not have any alternative model, the reliance on informal sector for borrowing has increased.

According to the Microfinance Network (MFIN) Report (July 2020), the loans disbursed by MFIs during the first quarter of 2020 are lower by a whopping 96% as compared with the last year (*The Financial Express* dated September 22, 2020). The pandemic followed by the lockdown has adversely impacted MSMEs and informal sector enterprises, and thus the MFI borrower segment. To revive the MFI sector, the government declared a series of relief measures including loan moratorium. However, banks are already facing problems and are cautious in extending the governmental measures and reluctant to dilute the norms because of the concern for increasing NPAs and weakening the entire system. This catch-22 problem does not have an instant solution. The book proposes a model that can be one of the many solutions for this problem.

As a silver lining in this dark situation, the use of UPI, mobile banking and government emphasis on cashless banking infrastructure have increased manyfold during the crisis. The outreach of banks and MFIs has contributed to the use of mobile banking in India, especially by the younger generation in rural and urban areas. As the volume of business increases, banks would have to take advantage of Fintech and resort to digital lending and even AI at a later date. The banks and financial sector can take advantage of this increased use of technology and acceptance of mobile banking by wider strata of population. By using digital lending, mobile banking and lean banking can reduce their transaction costs and increase their outreach.

We must realize that the pandemic is one of the many shocks in the history of an economic system. According to Nassim Taleb (*The New Yorker* dated April 21, 2020), these shocks are 'white swans' as these kind of events are not totally unknown and not impossible to happen in human history. Thus, the system should be ready to handle them in a resilient manner to prevent lesser damage. Thinkers, policy-makers, governments and practitioners must work towards building 'anti-fragile' systems in each field including banking. The primary goal of the system should be to achieve a reasonable degree of resilience so that crises like these do not rob one of one's minimum subsistence and dignity.

How can the banking system contribute to build this systemic resilience? These are times when it is essential for banks to 'challenge the conventional wisdom' (King, 2019) and explore innovative trajectory.

This book is an attempt to advocate one.

Inclusive Banking: An Economist's Approach

The authors perceive the above issues from an economist's perspective. It implies that the banking service is considered as a 'good'—a commodity traded in the financial markets with both demand side and supply side players. Banking as an industry provides this 'good'. The problem of providing this service to the poor arises for two reasons. First, banks as commercial firms operating in the free markets do not cater to poor customers. In the terminology of economics, the poor do not have effective demand backed by the purchasing power to avail of this service in the market. That is, they do not have assets or credit history to support their need for borrowing. Nor do they have surplus income to save in bank deposits.

Second, banking as a service is a quasi-social good because it creates positive externalities: society benefits if the poor can access finance, start saving and get loans for their enterprises. However, this does not happen naturally in commercial banking driven by the usual profit motives. The entire discussion around financial inclusion must revolve around the economics of financial inclusion.

Need to Redefine the Existing Model of Inclusive Banking

The narrative of financial inclusion needs a change. The existing dialogue on financial inclusion in the policy arena and academia abides by the viewpoint of bankers, regulators and policy-makers who are a part of the formal financial system. However, when zero balance accounts are opened but not used (*Global Findex Report*, 2017), and when more than 40% of the rural credit is from moneylenders (*All-India Debt and Investment Survey, 2012*), problems with this perspective become evident.

During the last few years, bank accounts have remained either inactive or underutilized because banks have not been motivated to take initiatives to implement microfinance schemes. Although they supported this segment indirectly over the years by financing microfinance institutions, they have never seriously considered nursing this clientele as their core customer base.

Those who are currently un-banked/under-utilizing bank accounts have been excluded because the particular model being followed caters to a privileged few. Hence, there is a need to redefine the model and make the entire population included.

A majority of the population is poor and requires microlending. The formal banking model is inadequate as it serves only a privileged minority. Hence, it becomes the responsibility of the traditionally formal system to adapt itself to service the population at large. We must note that the poor are not devoid of the banking services; rather, the banking system is devoid of them.

Why, then, do we need a new study on Inclusive Banking?

We see at least two valid reasons. First, in the vast pool of literature on financial inclusion, there exist few books that deal exclusively with inclusive banking. Our study aspires to be a comprehensive treatise on the subject. It discusses the problems of banking for the poor and proposes a new bank business model. Second, it is essential today for the volatility that exists in the financial sector has turned into an abysmal fear of the future of the economies—the future of market economy/capitalism. The black swan event of the global pandemic has shown the world how the vulnerability and helplessness of the poor are the ticking time bomb on which elitist systems stand. If left unaddressed, this can turn the socio-eco-political system upside down.

In most discussions on financial inclusion, the microfinance sector is often perceived as an appendage of the mainstream banking system. Banks' microfinance activities were reported as mere line items on annual financial statements. Further, in India, banks did not usually participate actively in microfinance lending operations.

This book obviously benefits from the previous studies, books and reports, but its essential postulation is that financing the poor should be the mainstream financing. The poor ought to be perceived as the 'regular' clientele upon which a financially feasible business model is built. In this endeavour, it addresses the broader spectrum of the entire financial inclusion ecosystem with banking as the underlying core sector for enhancing financial inclusion in India.

To what extent is the financial inclusion ecosystem successful in achieving its goal? Which element of this ecosystem is more efficient in providing access? What are the gaps and challenges that need attention? What is the role of banks as key stakeholders in this ecosystem? If, even after more than 50 years of effort at financial inclusion, we are still struggling for basic objectives like increasing the use of bank accounts by the poor in India and meeting their diverse financial needs, then how should the policy be reformed?

Post-PMJDY, the banks did not actively pursue to operationalize the PMJDY accounts. Urjit Patel, a former Governor of Reserve Bank of India, stated, 'My view about financial inclusion is probably different from that of my predecessors. Going forward I see that the market will take over this agenda through technology and innovation. The role of RBI will take a backseat' (Sriram, 2018). As suggested by Patel, after opening of the no frills accounts, the entire responsibility was left to the market. This has obviously not worked. The 'thin' files of such customers gather dust. Banks need to be proactive and to encourage these thin-filed customers to be in the system. It is essential that a special effort be made to get them in. While a business model ought to have been built earlier, we advocate remedial measures.

The book tries to offer a comprehensive view of these issues from perspectives of the stakeholders such that it will be useful to the practitioners, policy-makers and academics involved in the fields of banking, economics, finance, developmental policy and society. Financial inclusion is not a standalone policy. It is a part and parcel of the development policy aimed at alleviating poverty.

Why Are We Still Discussing Financial Inclusion Today?

At the Micro-level: The Persistence of Gaps in the Access to Banking Services Along with the Rising Aspirations of People

'Vahini, I want to buy a scooter so I can go even at a distance and earn more.'

Surekha, a domestic worker in Pune, tells her employer emphatically. She is a confident lady living in a *pucca* hut in one of the sprawling slums in the elite city of Pune.

A survey of 100 urban slum dwellers conducted by the authors in Pune showed that 23 of them did not have a bank account for varied reasons. Some of them lacked the necessary documentation. One slum dweller said, 'I don't need a bank account when I can live easily without one'. Almost all the members of self-help groups stated that they found it inconvenient to go to the bank for transactions and preferred to deal with the group members or relatives for monetary transactions.

When asked why they do not use an online bank account, respondents said that it was too complicated, too many questions were asked and too much paper work was involved. Additionally, most of the operations are in English.

We forget that microlending is not merely a loan disbursement exercise. The level of aspirations of these groups is rising in present times. Though the loans are largely for consumption, the latter is increasingly for upward mobility to cross class barriers. Interviews with the clients of MFIs reflect that they wanted loans in order to get better housing, their children's education and better means of communication. The requirements of the borrowers are changing. The microfinance borrowers are no longer limited to small consumption loans. They now demand larger loan than needed before for small businesses to effect upward mobility. Stalwart practitioners in the microfinance industry typically advocate bigger ticket size lending.

On the other hand, in spite of the fact that MFIs have been working for 25–30 years, many of their clients are still dependent on them for solving their existential problems.

At this juncture, one observes a mixed picture regarding the use of bank accounts and online banking in India. Figure 1.1 shows that the financial inclusion in India has improved in terms of the number of bank

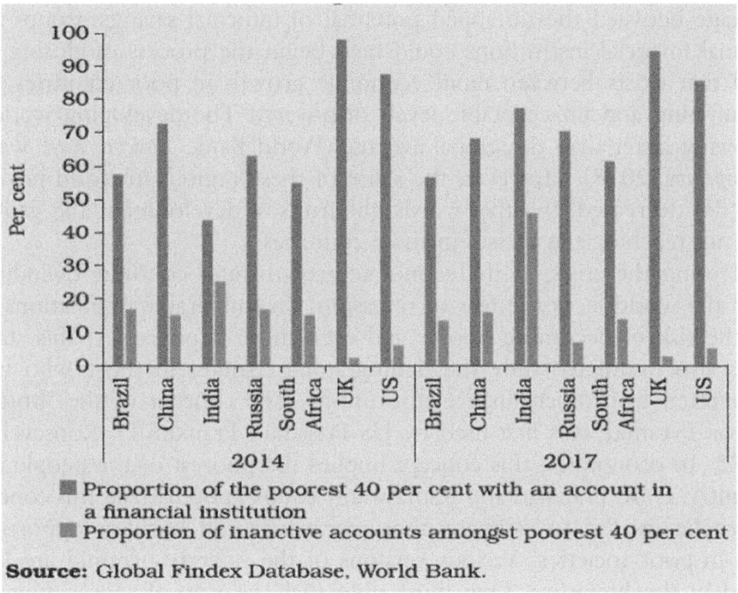

Fig. 1.1 Status of Financial Inclusion in India (*Source: Trends and Progress of Banking in India, 2018–19*, p. 64, The Global Findex Data, 2017)

accounts opened from 2015 to 2017. The official data claims that 40% are the poorest of the poor in India. Out of them, 77% have a bank account. Thus, India ranks at the top amongst BRICS countries in this regard. But one should not ignore the fact that the actual usage of accounts remains low (*Report on Trends and Progress of Banking in India, 2018–19*).

Empirical studies on financial inclusion are replete with such cases showing that bank-led financial inclusion in India has many gaps. If the financial inclusion were to be successful, it would have considered these aspirations as well as the needs, and the policy would have been redundant and we would not have to write about it anymore.

At Macro-level: The Importance of Financial Inclusion for Poverty Alleviation

Financial inclusion is regarded as a key channel to facilitate equitable distribution of resources. Finding policy solutions to enable greater linkage between the untapped potential of informal savings groups and formal financial institutions could help begin the process of closing the gap that exists between rapid economic growth in poor countries and continuing and unacceptable levels of poverty. The developing world is growing faster than the global average (World Bank, *Poverty and Shared Prosperity*, 2018). However, the share of these regions in world poverty has not decreased. In other words, the fruits of development and growth are not reaching the masses in these countries.

During the crisis, as the economic growth rates continue dwindling, and the world faces the fear of recession, the vulnerable populations are at the risk of becoming poorer and even more deprived. At this stage, it is also useful to study the demographic changes in those who have benefitted from microfinance institutions. The concept of the 'Bottom of the Pyramid' was first used by US President Franklin D. Roosevelt in 1932. In economics, this concept implies the poorest of the people in a country. C. K. Prahalad and Ramaswamy (2004) popularized this concept when he used it to estimate consumer needs and business opportunities in poor societies. Various versions of the poverty pyramid are later used in the literature. One must note that the way of segregating the population among three classes is not fixed. Many versions of the poverty pyramid have more classes like the non-poor class and the below subsistence level and above subsistence level class, etc. Figure 1.2 shows the poverty pyramid based on the 2011 estimates of poverty. For the purpose of inclusive finance, we can estimate that the banks and financial institutions should be able to cater at least to the population just at the margin above the subsistence level which is generally engaged in informal sector and casual employment. These are the people at the margin of poverty who are financially vulnerable and extreme shocks result in pushing them below the subsistence level of living. Inclusive banking has a great role to play in this segment.

The structure of the pyramid depends on the purpose for which it is used. The population in each level of the pyramid keeps on changing with the positive or negative shocks to the economy. For instance, after the pandemic, the economic slowdown and loss of jobs and earnings pushed a number of people at the margin from non-poor category to the poor category, and many from the poor category to the below subsistence level of living. According to the World Bank's *Poverty and Equity Brief on India* (April 2020), in India 176 million live in acute poverty and COVID-19 induced economic lock down has made the situation even worse. The

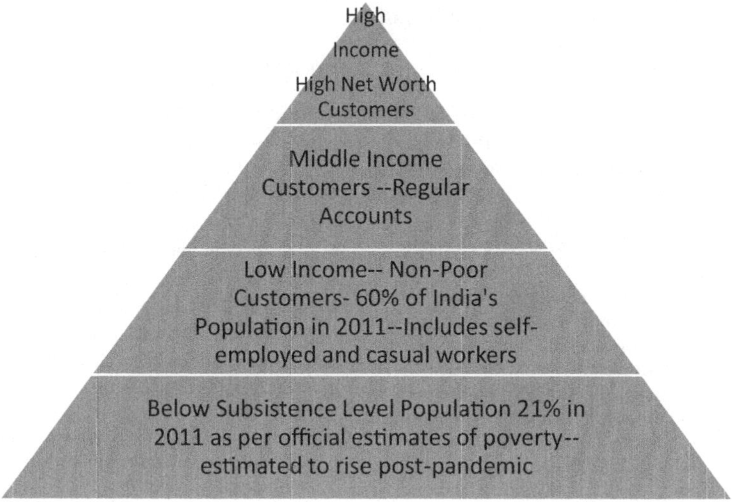

Fig. 1.2 India's Poverty Pyramid (*Source* Prepared by the authors based on *Poverty and Equity Brief* [World Bank, April 2020])

lock down and the economic slow down that followed have drastically reduced the incomes of the small business owners and temporary workers in petty shops, hotels, sundry businesses, etc. Government assistance is beneficial to only those who are in some way or the other included in the financial system by way of bank account ownership. Many poorest of the poor realized that they cannot avail of the governmental benefits as they have neither an account nor any official identity proof like a ration card or the Aadhaar card.

Where Does the Need for a Special Policy for Inclusive Banking Emerge?

The need for inclusive banking emerges from the existence of exclusion in financial activities. Why does this exclusion arise? The barriers to accessing finance for the poor are well documented in various reports and studies (Cull et al., 2012). Table 1.1 lists several demand side and supply side barriers mentioned in earlier studies (Rajan & Zingales, 2001; Beck et al., 2006; Dupas et al, 2012; Fuller & Mellor, 2008; Barr, 2004).

Table 1.1 Barriers to financial inclusion

Supply side barriers	*Demand side barriers*
• Lack of understanding or information of using mobile for account operations • Gender and age discrimination—research shows that women and young people are more likely to be excluded than others • Poor people's low income and erratic cash flow • Lack of suitable customized and schematic lending from formal financial service providers that cater to the needs of poor people • Proper usage of JAM like initiatives (digital lending) to reduce high transaction costs for banks to operate in remote locations as well as high transport and opportunity costs for people to bank with formal financial institutions • National and international policies that inhibit financial inclusion of the world's poorest people	• Need for liquidity and cash in hand leading to short-sighted view of repayment • Lack of awareness • Lack of education • Low income and no saving capacity • Lack of confidence and trust • Opportunity costs for people to bank with formal financial institutions • Lack of motivation to deal with unknown people in formal environment • Inertia to change from conventional informal sources of credit due to familiarity and comfort • Lack of marketing and bringing out features of schemes (like a provision for refund of interest after mortgaged loan is repaid)

Source Compiled by the authors

Table 1.1 lists common barriers across the developing world. In addition, there can be country-specific socio-cultural barriers like social norms regarding ownership and use of bank accounts and mobile accounts by women.

Socio-Cultural Dimensions of Gender Inequality in Financial Inclusion

In India, we have anecdotal evidence that women often want to keep their cash with their employers as their bank accounts are generally joint accounts with their spouses. Women are unsure whether their husbands will use the money for desirable purposes. In our survey, of slum dwellers in Pune,[1] one woman told us that she does not want the mobile app

[1] A field survey of 100 individuals residing in slums in Pune was undertaken by the authors during May to December 2019 to study the bank account ownership and mobile banking.

provided by her bank as her husband or son could withdraw from it without her knowledge.

Can New Models in Inclusive Banking Overcome These Barriers?

International experience shows that these barriers can be overcome with proper initiatives in inclusive banking. In Kenya and throughout sub-Saharan Africa, though a strong financial system does not exist, widespread use of mobile banking has facilitated financial inclusion. Some experimental initiatives were taken to break the barriers and make the poor use formal banking system. For instance, the *Banking on Change partnership* has reached 513,000 people in the African continent in three years. According to the report (2013), the estimated 2.5 billion unbanked people in South Africa can save annually $58 each on an average. Thus, $145 billion are lost to the economy if these savings are not mobilized. Banking the unbanked is important not only for the poor but also for the economy.

These kinds of initiatives should be studied to examine their replicability and scalability across countries. The Fintech revolution has great potential to overcome these barriers, and by building an extensive Fintech infrastructure, banks would be able to do away with the conventional barriers of microfinance.

One of our purposes is to discuss the changes that can be brought about in the inclusive banking business model that is scalable and replicable across India.

Before delving into the potential inclusive banking model, it is necessary to define inclusive banking. The following part of the chapter defines inclusive banking and provides an overview of the recent trends in financial inclusion.

Defining Inclusive Banking

India's tryst with inclusivity in banking began in 1969 with the nationalization of commercial banks. But surprisingly, an official definition of *inclusive banking* is unavailable in banking regulations and literature. It is mistaken to be identical to *financial inclusion*. Since the discussion about *financial inclusion* is available in the literature, it has to be verified whether financial inclusion needs to be differentiated from *inclusive banking*. Therefore, we discuss the definition of financial inclusion as the starting point in the process of defining inclusive banking.

Existing Definition(s) of Financial Inclusion and Financial Inclusion Universe

Since the nationalization of banks, financial inclusion in India is typically practised through priority sector lending by banks. However, the term was formally coined by Y. V. Reddy, ex- Governor, Reserve Bank of India, in 2005 (Joshi, 2013). He called out banks for adopting banking practices that lead to exclusion of larger sections of population. The main features of the approach involve 'connecting' people with the banking system and not just focusing on credit. As stated by Thorat (2007), 'Financial exclusion can be thought of in two ways, one is exclusion from the payments system, i.e., not having access to a bank account and the second type of exclusion is from formal credit markets requiring the excluded to approach informal and exploitive markets'.

After 2005, the literature is flooded with the definitions and studies on financial inclusion.

In India, various committees addressing financial inclusion have defined financial inclusion in broad terms. For instance, the Committee on Financial Inclusion under the chairmanship of C. Rangarajan (2008) defined financial inclusion as 'the process of ensuring access to financial services and timely and adequate credit where needed by vulnerable groups such as weaker sections and low-income groups at an affordable cost'.

The Committee on Financial Sector Reforms (2013), chaired by Raghuram Rajan, stated, 'Financial Inclusion, broadly defined, refers to universal access to a wide range of financial services at a reasonable cost. These include not only banking products, but also other financial services such as insurance and equity products'.

The Rajan Committee report (2009) mentioned, 'Instead of seeing the issue primarily as expanding credit, which puts the cart before the horse, we urge a refocus to seeing it (financial inclusion) as expanding access to financial services, such as payments services, savings products, insurance products, and inflation-protected pensions' (p. 6). The Nachiket Mor Committee (2014) defined financial inclusion as the spread of financial institutions and financial services across the country. It further adds that financial inclusion can be said to be complete only when there is access to a suite of appropriate products and services for all the financial needs of a household or enterprise. Households planning for long-term goals such as retirement require inflation-adjusted returns on investment over substantial time periods.

The report of the Committee on Medium-term Path on Financial Inclusion (Mohanty, 2015, p. 23) states, 'Financial inclusion [is] broadly understood as access to the formal financial sector for the marginalized and formal-finance deprived sections of society'. It also pointed out that the access and use of bank accounts can be now 'seamlessly integrated' with the help of Jan Dhan, Aadhaar and Mobile (JAM) trinity. It visualized efficient interoperability across various institutions through technological innovations, mobile wallet and e-money to increase the use of cashless transactions.

The recent National Strategy for Financial Inclusion NSFI Report (2019) articulates a five-year (2019–2024) vision and key objectives of financial inclusion policies in India. It visualizes financial inclusion as an access to a broad spectrum of financial services. The strategy is depicted in Fig. 1.3. Launched in August 2014, it was a watershed in the financial inclusion movement in the country. The programme leverages the existing large banking network and technological innovations to provide

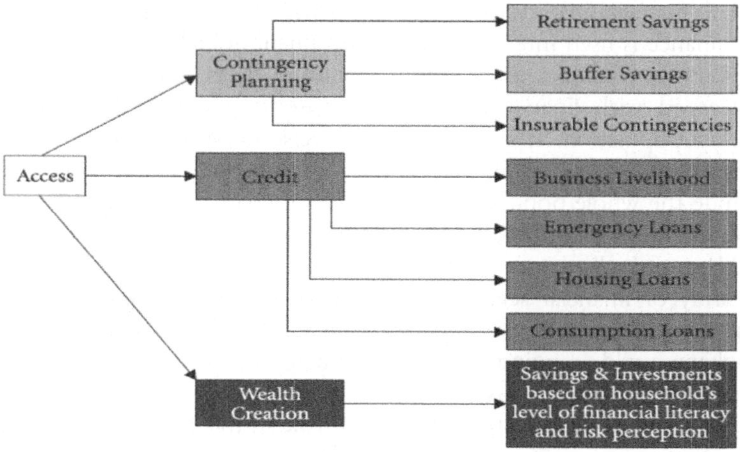

Fig. 1.3 Household access to financial services (*Source* India Incomes and Savings Survey, IISS, 2007)

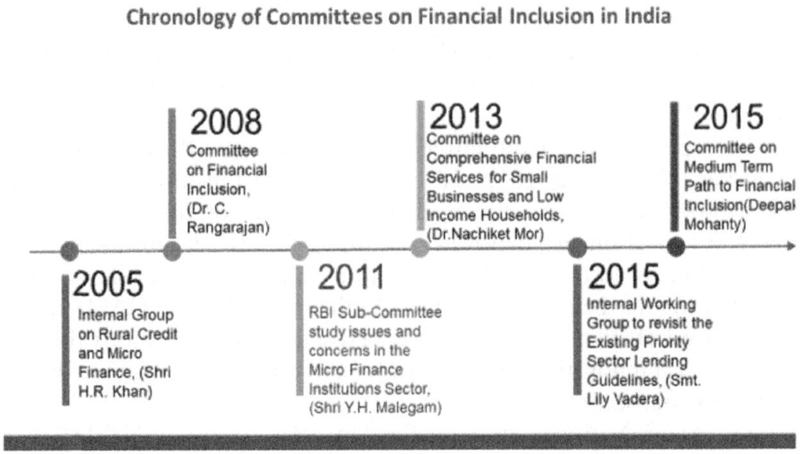

Fig. 1.4 Chronology of committees on financial inclusion in India (*Source* Compiled by the authors)

every household with access to basic financial services, thereby bridging the gap in the coverage of banking facilities (NSFI, 2019, p. 8).[2]

Thus, the term financial inclusion involves the entire financial sector and all financial institutions and instruments. Sometimes the term inclusive finance is used interchangeably with financial inclusion.

Inclusive finance: It is often confused with microfinance. It is concerned with financial services and products designed to aid low-income population. It is broader but precise because it regroups all the activities linked to the financial sector, but also indicates its objective to include the whole population irrespective of income, gender, caste, class, race and religion in the economic system.

Most of the literature on inclusive finance defines it in terms of making an array of financial services accessible to low-income segment of the population. The inclusive finance or financial inclusion is a broad term involving a wide-ranging spectrum of financial services and diverse institutional ecosystem. Thus, it is necessary to delimit the term inclusive banking and to demarcate its scope and role in this broader framework.

[2] Chapter 6 of this book provides a detailed discussion on Government's initiatives on inclusive banking.

In the absence of an official definition, inclusive banking has to be defined as the financial inclusion practised by banks. It has never been defined officially by any act or committee in India. It will be seen that, in this book, instead of using broader terms like inclusive finance and financial inclusion, we deliberately use the term inclusive banking.

Inclusive banking can be defined as the business of banking done by a banking company, as defined in the Banking Regulation Act of 1949, by implementing the principles of financial inclusion.

Definition of Inclusive Banking and Its Ideological Implications

This simple and logical definition of inclusive banking comes with a complex ideological and practical weight. It combines a development concept (inclusive) with a commercial concept (banking).

Thus, inclusive banking is financial inclusion in banking services. However, the social mandate in banking gives rise to a debate on whether commercial banks should adopt social or development goals. In India, the social mandate was integrated into the banking functions of the public sector banks, as they have been given the responsibility of implementing developmental goals of the government.

This leads us to the ideological debate on the desirability of commercial banks being asked to undertake the priority sector lending and the developmental goals in the first place. Chapter 2 of this book delves into the theoretical underpinnings of this conflict.

Inclusive Banking—Global Approach

Globally, a formal approach to financial inclusion can be traced to the United Nations' initiatives articulated through the famous 'Building Inclusive Financial Sectors for Development' or the Blue Book (2006). This detailed vision of inclusive finance described inclusive finance in terms of making accessible a broad range of financial services to all *bankable* households and enterprises at a reasonable cost.

Formal and global level evolution of inclusive banking can be traced to the World Bank's adoption of financial inclusion as an enabler for 7 of the 17 Sustainable Development Goals. The World Bank put forward the access to finance as one of its world development goals. This prompted policy-makers and regulators in various countries to actively plan and strategize policy initiatives in this regard. It defined financial inclusion as individuals and businesses having access to useful and affordable financial products and services that meet their needs—transactions, payments, savings, life style saving schemes, credit and housing finance which are delivered in a responsible and sustainable way.

Since the World Bank Group identified financial inclusion as a key enabler in reducing extreme poverty and boosting shared prosperity, policy-makers have explicitly included it in their macroeconomic policy goals. Governments have been making policy efforts for inclusive banking as evident from community banking in USA; or bank nationalization, establishment of regional rural banks and priority sector lending in India.

Community Banking: It facilitates financial inclusion in the USA. Since 1977, the Community Reinvestment Act (1977) made it mandatory for the banks to offer lending to a broader area without just targeting the richer population. Community banks are smaller in size than the commercial banks and they primarily serve the community where they are located. Their lending is based on relationship banking and they primarily cater to small businesses. They fill in the gaps in financial services by providing credit to rural and small businesses. Community banks are important in financial inclusion in USA but are declining in number after the mergers (Kahn et al., 2003). In Germany, the 'Everyman' banking account is aimed at catering to the basic customer similar to the BSBDA in India. Similarly, the low cost bank account called 'Mzansi' exists in South Africa. The need for a regulatory framework ensuring safety of the consumer is emphasized by the G20 Toronto Summit (June 2010). The principles for smooth adoption of innovative models for reducing the costs and ensuring financial feasibility of inclusive finance for institutions in mainstream finance like banks and insurance companies and financial inclusion policy at international level have been laid down by this summit.

Thus, the evolution of financial inclusion in various countries including India has been characterized by initial policy thrust by the regulatory authorities, legislature, government policies and commercial banks.

Scope of Inclusive Banking

The scope of inclusive banking could be based on the primary banking functions. A bank being an intermediary between the surplus and deficit units in the economy, these functions are deposit mobilization and credit provision. In this sense, inclusive banking is the act of undertaking banking functions in an inclusive manner.

It involves banks actively facilitating financial awareness, rural entrepreneurship and providing support in developmental schemes for poverty alleviation.[3]

It is closely integrated with financial inclusion though the latter is a much broader concept going beyond regular banking operations. Even if we define its scope to include only regular banking activities, the financial inclusion agenda cannot be isolated from it, as the universal access to basic banking services is the first step towards financial inclusion.

As specified in the World Bank's goals for Universal Financial Access, inclusive banking aims at providing a bank account to unbanked adult individuals so that they can participate in payment transactions and use these accounts for their financial needs (*Universal Financial Access 2020, 2018*).

Globally, the adoption of a formal National Financial Inclusion Strategy (NFIS) has accelerated significantly in the past decade (World Bank Group, 2018).

Evolution of Inclusive Banking in India

The evolution of inclusive banking in India is reviewed from three perspectives: (1) the committees established for analysis of financial inclusion; (2) the reforms and initiatives actually implemented in this area; and (3) the actual progress of inclusive banking.

Inclusive Banking - Overview of Recommendations by Various Committees Since 2000

This section provides an overview of the journey of financial inclusion in India through the formulation and recommendations of various committees.

The official definition of financial inclusion and an explicit strategy for financial inclusion was evolved by the Internal Group on Rural Credit and

[3]The literature most commonly identifies the exclusion from financial system on account of low incomes. However, the exclusion on account of caste, colour, race, gender, etc., is not widely analysed except for a few studies on gender disparity and caste biases in the financial system.

Microfinance in 2005. In 2006, the Government of India constituted a Committee on Financial Inclusion which made wide-ranging recommendations for making Indian financial sector inclusive for both urban and rural areas. In recent times, the strategy of financial inclusion is steered by the Financial Stability and Development Council (FSDC) of the Government of India. Various committees have identified specific gaps in the contemporary financial inclusion framework. An overview of the major recommendations gives an idea of the course of financial inclusion in India.[4]

1. Internal Group on Rural Credit and Microfinance, 2005 (H. R. Khan), recommended the Business Facilitator and Business Correspondent Model. It stated that the banks should appoint business correspondents and facilitators for expanding banking services beyond the brick and mortar offices.
2. In 2008, the Committee on Financial Inclusion chaired by C. Rangarajan recommended that banks should undertake branch expansion in certain identified districts and can use primary agricultural cooperatives and NBFCs as business correspondents. It also suggested that a National Rural Financial Inclusion Plan should be prepared along with a demarcated financial inclusion fund. These recommendations were eventually implemented by the RBI and it was ensured that each village has at least one bank branch. In 2010, banks were required to formulate three year financial inclusion plans and a financial inclusion fund was also created.
3. The recommendations of the RBI Sub-Committee of its Central Board of Directors to study issues and concerns in the Microfinance Institutions Sector, 2011 (Chairman, Y. H. Malegam), were important as the microfinance sector went through an infamous crisis during 2010. The Committee recommended restructuring the microfinance sector and provided a regulatory framework. According to it, the MFIs that typically catered to low-income borrowers were classified into a new category of NBFC MFIs. The

[4]The following discussion on committees and their recommendations is drawn from Joshi, D. P. (2013). Financial Inclusion: Journey So Far and Road Ahead. Speech delivered by Executive Director, RBI, at the Mint Conclave on Financial Inclusion on November 28.

latter were covered under the RBI regulation. This helped in formalizing and streamlining the microfinance sector to protect the interest of the low-income borrowers. The composition of the sector and related issues is discussed in Chapter 4.

4. In 2013, the Committee on Comprehensive Financial Services for Small Businesses and Low Income Households, 2013 (Chairman Nachiket Mor), widened the gamut of financial inclusion policy. It suggested changes related to the use of digitalization and electronic finance give universal access to financial services in microlending.

   The recommendations of these committees were implemented by the RBI and thus progress was achieved in terms of increase in the number of bank accounts, number of bank branches and coverage of unbanked villages.

   The range of financial services offered to the low-income groups was also widened. The RBI created payment banks and small finance banks.

5. In 2015, Internal Working Group to Revisit the Existing Priority Sector Lending Guidelines, 2015 (headed by Lily Vadera), expanded the definition of priority sector to include medium enterprises and renewable energy, and specified sub-targets of priority sector lending to small and marginal farmers, and microenterprises.
6. The importance of digital finance has been recognized by the Committee on Medium Term Path to Financial Inclusion chaired by Deepak Mohanty. It stressed the importance of direct cash transfer by the government and gender parity in account opening through Sukanya Shiksha Scheme. It recommended that Aadhaar cards should be linked to each individual credit account as a unique biometric identifier. This step can be crucial for reducing the costs of monitoring thin-filed borrowers. The Committee also recommended the use of mobile technology to improve the last mile service delivery by the banks.

> Its recommendations have been forward-looking to manage the problems of inclusive banking through digitalization. Direct social benefit transfer has been implemented during the pandemic cash benefit transfer. This has the double welfare effect of preventing corruption and encouraging the low-income segment to own bank accounts. The Committee also suggested some other measures like

doing away with agriculture interest subvention scheme, crop insurance for small and marginal farmers, use of credit bureaus for MSMEs, etc.

Evolution of Inclusive Banking in India—The Initiatives

In India, much before the formal adoption of the financial inclusion objective, the financial inclusion policy has been implemented through various initiatives like bank nationalization, regional rural banks, agricultural cooperatives, self-help groups, etc. (K. C. Chakrabarty, 2011). In fact, even before the nationalization of banks in 1969, India had nationalized the life insurance companies in 1956 (*National Strategy for Financial Inclusion, 2019*).

RBI Initiatives for Inclusive Banking Since 2005

Figure 1.5 depicts important initiatives undertaken by the RBI for inclusive banking in India from 1969 to 2018. According to the *National*

Fig. 1.5 Chronology of RBI Initiatives for Inclusive Banking (*Source* Compiled by the authors)

Financial Inclusion Strategy Report (2019),[5] the financial inclusion policy rests on the bank-led model. The targets of financial inclusion are defined in terms of branch expansion and bank account ownership. Banks are the primary channels of implementing financial inclusion policy. This is a natural choice because firstly, India has a bank-led economy and secondly, the regulator can closely monitor the progress of inclusion in terms of banking indicators. Thus, banks were responsible for the progress of financial inclusion from time to time. They expanded their branches to the unbanked villages, lended to the priority sector, refinanced the NBFC MFIs and the cooperative banks, appointed BCs and opened BSBDAs. After the launch of the PMJDY and PMMY schemes, the focus of inclusive banking has been on their implementation by banks, associated with MFIs and SHGs.

Evolution and Progress of Inclusive Banking in India—The Performance

The following discussion provides an overview of the evolution and progress of inclusive banking in India based on selected parameters which specifically refer to the RBI initiatives for bank-led financial inclusion.

Total rural banking outlets increased from 67.7 thousand in 2008–2009 to 597 thousand in 2018–2019. However, the growth in banking outlets in villages with a population of less than 2000 has been slow as compared with their growth in rural areas.

The growth in no frills accounts has increased exponentially after the introduction of the PMJDY in 2014. The growth rate of ATMs also shows a greater increase after 2014–2015.

Bank-led financial inclusion has been the policy focus after the JAM.

The Current Landscape of Inclusive Finance in India

Market structure can be explained in terms of the topology of the entire ecosystem as inclusive banking does not exist in isolation and is linked with microfinance and SHG activities. On the supply side are

[5] https://rbidocs.rbi.org.in/rdocs/content/pdfs/NSFIREPORT100119.pdf. Accessed 25 March 2020.

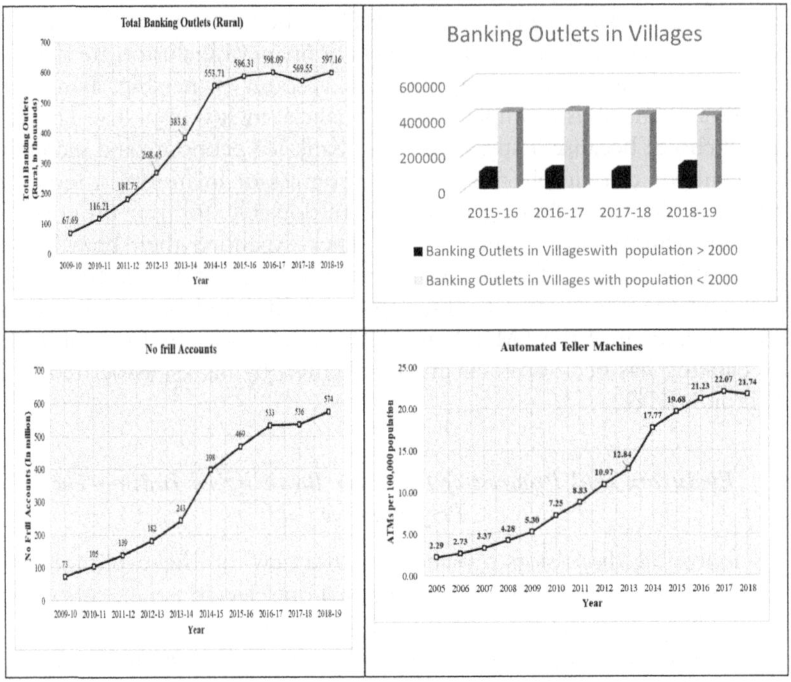

Fig. 1.6 Progress of inclusive banking in India—Selected parameters (*Source* Compiled by the authors from the RBI, STRBI and the World Bank database)

banks, microfinance institutions, SHGs and the government, while on the demand side are the consumers of inclusive finance and banking who form the households in need of this service.

The supply side structure of this market is evolving. The number of players in the market is a primary factor that influences the behaviour of the participants. This market has grown over the decades. The total number of SHGs is 65,49,518 as reported by the NRLM website of GOI, while the *Status of Microfinance Report 2018-19* by NABARD reports 1 crore SHGs. The number of MFIs is 223 according to the *MFIN report* in March 2020. Thus, the market structure has become competitive. This is reflected in the provision of services by the MFIs and SHGs.

Banks directly implement the inclusive schemes like PMJDY and PMMY. They also play an indirect role by financially supporting SHGs and MFIs. Since only the SHGs, NGOs and MFIs are active in the field, the poor end up thinking that only these non-bank institutions help them. As a result, banks never get direct credit for the progress of financial inclusion. In fact, in the current pandemic scenario, banks bear the financial burden of implementing various government schemes from loan waivers to moratoriums on loan repayment.

Current Policy—Paternalistic Approach[6]

The inclusive banking policy in India began from the paternalistic initiative of bank nationalization. It reflected state paternalism as it directed banks about whom to lend and incentivized the people for productive borrowing. It implied that the government knows how best to use the nation's capital resources.

Banking: Social or Commercial?

Since bank nationalization, the debate continues whether it is desirable for a commercial bank to have social goals. Various committees (Narsimham Committee, 1991, 1998) have critically looked at the effect of social sector lending on the profitability of banks.

Inclusivity in banking requires that the inclusive policy must be financially feasible and profitable for the banking firms. Lack of profitability leads to unsustainable business, while lack of conviction in profitability in business will lead to its failure.

Banks were misused and abused by the government in later years for financing fiscal deficit. This was criticized from the early 1980s. The two Narsimham Committees recommended liberalization of banks (from government fiscal policy!). They criticized priority sector lending norms, regulated interest rates and fiscal burden on banks. Liberalization of the banking sector with increased competition, less regulation and free interest rates was recommended to improve bank profitability and efficiency. These recommendations were implemented partially. As a result, on the one hand, banks face competition and liberalization in some areas like deregulation of interest rates while, on the other, they bear the

[6] In Esther Duflo's Marshall Lecture Sense. Duflo, Esther (2013), Paternalism, Freedom, and Hope in the Fight Against Poverty, Marshal Lecture 2012–13, University of Cambridge.

financial burden of government's domestic borrowing, loan waivers and government schemes. By 2018–2019, the RBI nudged banks to be independent. In 2019, bank restructuring was announced with their mega mergers. In early 2020, the government-aided private banks in coming out of financial debacles. This schizophrenic policy environment, coupled with external forces of global trade wars, corporate bankruptcies, loan defaults, recession and economic slowdown due to pandemic, has made the entire sector fragile. At this juncture, a paradigm shift with a fresh perspective on banking business is imperative for the survival and the revival of the banking sector.

Banking for the Poor Matters—Need to Change the Narrative

Business models of banks are not developed to include the poor as their client base.

The bankers treated it apart. To incorporate it into their business model, they had to be open and agile.

K. C. Chakrabarty categorically stated, 'We have been very clear that banks must take up financial inclusion as a viable business. Let banks prove that this is not a viable business activity for them. We have always maintained that financial inclusion and removal of poverty cannot happen unless these are done in a viable manner. It cannot be done as a charity' (*The Economic Times*, April 14, 2014).

We are still discussing financial inclusion after more than fifty years of bank nationalization because banks have never perceived the poor as their clientele. They do not perceive providing loans to and accepting deposits from the poor as a viable business. Hence, they follow the policy initiatives and government directives apathetically. From a banker's perspective, profitable business is found outside the social sector. Hence, all the products are targeted at the regular 'profitable' clientele. All banks, private and public alike, compete for this regular business and are therefore geographically concentrated. Clustered bank branches on main roads in any bustling city, e.g. Veera Desai Road in Andheri West (Mumbai); Rajiv Chowk (New Delhi); and M G Road (Nasik) are glaring examples of this mindless competition.

The recent pandemic and consequent economic crisis have reminded us that a vast majority of India's population has unstable and low incomes. Banks should realize that a business model focused on a higher income population is not sustainable in a country where the majority is poor and has low and unstable incomes due to seasonal employment and, in turn, lacks assets. At the same time, the social banking approach of serving the poor for social or charitable purposes is not consistent with economic logic as is evident from the past experience. Inclusive banking will be effective only if it has a potential to be a viable business strategy. The present economic situation is characterized by high NPAs from high-income clients, abysmally low industrial growth and lower interest rates. In this situation, banks can no longer depend on the existing business model for their survival. Banking for the poor can provide a promising alternate business model in this situation. They should explore the possibilities of developing new business models based on the vast client pool of the low-income population. The poor have sustained without banks. Today, the question is: Can the banks survive without serving them?

References

Allan, A., Massu, M., & Svarer, C. (2013). Banking on change: Breaking barriers to financial inclusion. *Plan, Barclays and Care, 32.*

Barr, M. S. (2004, September). *Banking the poor: Policies to bring low-income Americans into financial mainstream* (Research Brief). Brookings Institution.

Beck, T., Demirguc-Kunt, A., & Martinez Peria, M. S. (2006). *Banking services for everyone? Barriers to bank access and use around the world.* The World Bank.

Chakrabarty, K. C. (2011, October 14). *Address at the FICCI (Federation of Indian Chambers of Commerce & Industry) – UNDP (The United Nations Development Programme Seminar on "Financial Inclusion: Partnership between Banks, MFIs and Communities"*. New Delhi.

Chakrabarty, K. C. (2014, April 14). Interview with *The Economic Times*. Retrieved from https://economictimes.indiatimes.com/opinion/interviews/reserve-bank-of-india-must-end-discretionary-regulation-k-c-chakrabarty-deputy-governor-rbi.

Cull, R., Demirguc-Kunt, A., & Morduch, J. (2012). *Banking the world: Empirical foundations of financial inclusion.* Massachusetts Institute of Technology,

Day, G. S., et al. (2004). Invited commentaries on "evolving to a new dominant logic for marketing". *Journal of Marketing, 68*(1), 18–27.

Demirgüç-Kunt, A., Klapper, L., Singer, D., Ansar, S., & Hess, J. (2018). *The Global Findex database 2017: Measuring financial inclusion and the Fintech Revolution.* Washington, DC: World Bank. https://doi.org/10.1596/978-1-4648-1259-0. License: Creative Commons Attribution CC BY 3.0 IGO.

Demirguc-Kunt, A., Martinez Peria, M. S., & Aggarwal, R. (2006). *Do workers' remittances promote financial development?*

Duflo, E. (2013). *Paternalism, freedom, and hope in the fight against poverty, Marshal Lecture 2012–13.* University of Cambridge. Retrieved from https://www.econ.cam.ac.uk/Marshall_Lecture/ML-past-lectures.html.

Dupas, P., Green, S., Keats, A., & Robinson, J. (2012). *Challenges in banking the rural poor: Evidence from Kenya's western province* (No. w17851). National Bureau of Economic Research.

Financial Express, Dated 22 September 2020. https://www.financialexpress.com/industry/banking-finance/micro-loans-disbursement-falls-96-in-q1-as-borrowers-struggle-for-livelihood-amid-pandemic-bank-credit-repo-rate/2089251/.

Fuller, D., & Mellor, M. (2008). Banking for the poor: addressing the needs of financially excluded communities in Newcastle upon Tyne. *Urban Studies, 45*(7), 1505–1524.

IISS Survey. (2007). *Invest India Income and Savings Survey 2007*. Invest India Economic Foundation Private Limited.

Kahn, G. A., Schroeder, L., Weiner, S., Keeton, W., Harvey, J., & Willis, P. (2003). The role of community banks in the US economy. *Economic Review (Kansas City), 88*(2), 15–44.

King, M. (2019, October 19). *Per Jacobsson Lecture, Delivered at the IMF Annual Meetings*.

Mohanty, D. (2015). *Report of the committee on medium-term path on financial inclusion*. Reserve Bank of India, 1–102.

Mor, N. (2014). *Comprehensive financial services for small businesses and low income households*.

NABARD. (2019). *Status of Microfinance Report, (2018–19)*. NABARD. Retrived from https://www.nabard.org/auth/writereaddata/tender/1207192354SMFI%202018-19.pdf.

Narasimham, M. (1998). *Report of the committee on banking sector reforms, April 1998*.

Narsimham, M. (1991). *The Committee on financial System*. Nabhi Publication.

NSSO. (2012). *Key indicators of debt and investment in India*. National Sample Survey Organization. Retrieved from https://mospi.gov.in/sites/default/files/publication_reports/KI_70_18.2_19dec14.pdf.

Prahalad, C. K., & Ramaswamy, V. (2004). *Co-creating unique value with customers*. Strategy & leadership.

Qoshi, D. P. (2013, November 28). *Financial inclusion: Journey so far and Road ahead*. Speech delivered by Executive Director, RBI at the Mint Conclave on Financial Inclusion.

Rajan, R. (2009). *A hundred small steps*. Report of the Committee on Financial sector reforms (Planning Commission Government of India): 50–53.

Rajan, R. G., & Zingales, L. (2001). Financial systems, industrial structure, and growth. *Oxford Review of Economic Policy, 17*(4), 467–482.

RBI. (2005). *Draft report of the internal group to examine issues relating to rural credit and microfinance, Chairman, HR Khan*. Retrieved from https://rbidocs.rbi.org.in/rdocs/PublicationReport/Pdfs/63448.pdf.

RBI. (2008). Report of the committee on financial inclusion. *Ministry of Finance, Government of India* (Chairman: Rangarajan, C.).

RBI. (2011). *Report of the sub-committee of the Central Board of Directors of Reserve Bank of India to study issues and concerns in the MFI sector*. Malegam, S.Y.H. Reserve Bank of India. New Delhi.

RBI. (2012). *Report of the internal working group to revisit the existing priority sector lending guidelines (Chairman Lily Vadera)*. Retrieved from https://www.rbi.org.in/scripts/BS_PressReleaseDisplay.aspx?prid=33360.

RBI. (2013). *A hundred small steps: Report of the committee on financial sector reforms (Chairman: Rajan, R. G.)*. Retrieved from https://www.rbi.org.in/scripts/AnnualPublications.aspx?head=Trend%20and%20Progress%20of%20Banking%20in%20India.

RBI. (2018). *Report on trends and progress of banking in India, RBI, (2018–19)*.

RBI. (2019). *National Strategy for Financial Inclusion (2019–24)*. Retrived from https://rbidocs.rbi.org.in/rdocs/content/pdfs/NSFIREPORT100119.pdf.

Sriram, M. S. (2018). *Talking financial inclusion in liberalised India: Conversations with governors of Reserve Bank of India*. Routledge.

The New Yorker. Interview by Prof. Nassim Taleb. Retrieved from https://www.newyorker.com/news/daily-comment/the-pandemic-isnt-a-black-swan-but-a-portent-of-a-more-fragile-global-system.

Thorat, U. (2007). *Financial inclusion—The Indian experience*. Speech at the HMT-DFID Financial Inclusion Conference 2007, London, 19 June 2007, BIS Review, 71/2007.

United Nations Capital Development Fund. (2006). *Building inclusive financial sectors for development*. United Nations Publications.

United Nations Committee on Trade and Development. (2020, May 14). *How COVID-19 is changing the world: A statistical perspective*. Geneva. Retrieved from https://unstats.un.org/unsd/ccsa/documents/covid19-report-ccsa.pdf.

World Bank Group. (2018). *Developing and operationalizing a national financial inclusion strategy*. World Bank Group.

World Bank Group. (2020). *Universal Financial Access 2020* (2018, October 09). Retrieved from World Bank Website: https://www.worldbank.org/en/topic/financialinclusion/brief/achieving-universal-financial-accessby-2020. https://ufa.worldbank.org/.

World Bank Report. (2019). https://www.worldbank.org/en/news/press-release/2019/06/04/global-growth-to-weaken-to-26-in-2019-substantial-risks-seen.

CHAPTER 2

Inclusive Finance and Economic Growth: The Theoretical Underpinnings

Inclusive finance is defined as the strategy of providing financial services to the poor and deprived sections of the population. This strategy may interfere with the profit maximization goal of the financial intermediaries. Inclusive finance necessitates government intervention and thus, generates an argument over whether intervention is desirable or not. Adopting a theoretical perspective on inclusive banking is important to have a precise view and conceptual understanding of the banks' role in the economy beyond their microeconomic stature as business entities. Banks as business firms are commercial institutions providing credit in the credit markets. The lending decision about whether to advance credit to borrowers is essentially based on the repayment capacity of the borrowers reflected by their net worth. Inclusive banking by definition requires the lender to provide credit and financial services to the poor at affordable costs. The ideological issue of whether the financial intermediaries should stick to their profit maximizing objective or they should serve the social objective of providing finance is rooted in the welfare economics theory.

A major portion of the literature on financial inclusion consists of empirical studies establishing the relation between inclusive finance and economic growth. Theorizing this relationship is essential because theory helps to establish the general applicability and predictability of this nexus between inclusive finance and economic growth. Both theory and empirics are essential for vigorous development of any research

L. Kulkarni and V. C. Joshi, *Inclusive Banking In India*,
https://doi.org/10.1007/978-981-33-6797-5_2

area. Theoretical treatment of the relation between inclusive finance and growth will help in designing future policy initiatives. Using the evaluation of these initiatives with empirical techniques (like randomized controlled trials) refines initiatives and this, in turn, helps to extend our theoretical understanding.

Where does finance and financial inclusion fit in the framework of economic theory? Do various economic theories of welfare, development and public policy justify inclusive banking? Do the theories help policymakers solve the ideological problem of whether the banks should better act as commercial profit maximizing institutions or they should meet the needs of the society? The following sections try to delve into these theoretical underpinnings of inclusive banking.

Inclusive Finance in Theory of Economic Growth and Development

To discuss 'inclusive' finance in the theory of growth and development, one has to initially consider how this theory perceives financial sector and its role in economic growth and development of a country.

Finance - a Black Sheep of Macroeconomic Theory?

According to various economic theories of growth and development, the real factors like labour and capital endowments, technology, exports and imports are drivers of growth. The classical theory of money dismisses the role of money by treating it as a 'veil' and thus completely ignores the role of credit and finance in the functioning of an economy. In Keynes' theory, financial markets were scorned off as casinos or beauty contests. The post-Keynesian and neo-classical economists also ignored the role of financial sector. The macroeconomists regarded real sector activities as the core of economies while finance just followed as a fall out of real sector activity and nothing more (Joan Robinson, 1952) and its role in economic growth might not be 'overstressed' (Lucas, 1988, p. 6; Levine, 2005).

Thus, the traditional economic models do not recognize the role of financial sector in the process of economic growth while the modern economists disagree sharply about its role in economic growth.

Development economics does not recognize the role of finance (Meier & Seers, 1984).

According to Miller (1998), the contribution of financial markets for growth is too obvious for serious discussion. Many economists recognize the role of finance as the carrier of capital and thus do not agree that one can completely disregard the interconnection between financial sector and economic growth in analysing how the economies grow (Levine, 2005).

Ignored by Theory but Redeemed by Empirical Evidence

Economic theory does not recognize the role of finance and financial sector in economic development. As finance is not important for economic growth, similarly whether it is inclusive or not, does not matter for economic growth as the latter depends on factors like production, technology and external sector. Correspondingly, the role of financial inclusion also is completely ignored by theory as a determinant factor in economic development.

In contrast, empirical studies show a clear and consistent relation between financial inclusion and growth across the countries. Demirgüç-Kunt and Levine (2004) discuss this role in empirical literature. As stated by Levine (2005), 'Macroeconomic models of growth and development are starkly oblivious of the role of financial inclusion in the process of economic development'. Although empirical methodologies are contestable, with more advanced econometric techniques and better data availability, the relation between financial inclusion and growth is manifested with more consistency in recent times. This is shown by recent empirical studies (Demirgüç-Kunt et al., 2017). Studies in the last couple of decades examine the importance of banks for lending to small businesses. Petersen and Rajan (1994) found that small businesses get easier access to lending through relationship banking. Many a time firms get benefits like lower lending rates and no collateral requirements if they have a long-run relationship with the institutional lender (Berger & Udell, 1995). The studies based on data from various countries examine relation between financial inclusion and GDP growth rates, economic development and lower income inequality. Almost all these studies show that financial inclusion leads to better economic growth and lower inequality (King & Levine, 1993; Beck et al., 2000; Clark et al., 2003; Demirguc-Kunt et al., 2017).

While the empirical studies prove the role of financial sector and contribution of financial inclusion in economic growth, some issues remain unanswered in these studies. For instance, the justification for government interventionist policy to bring about financial intermediaries to implement inclusive business strategy and inability of the markets to cater efficiently to the needs of the poor are not satisfactorily dealt with without a theoretical exposition.

Theories provide alternative theoretical arguments to justify policy interventions by the government in the free credit markets.

Rationale for Inclusive Banking Policy—Multiple Theoretical Perspectives

If the markets are not capable of achieving financial inclusion, then government intervention is needed. Rationale for inclusive banking policy can be found in various economic theories and/or their critiques. The theoretical underpinnings of inclusive finance can be categorized into three approaches. First is the welfare economics approach based on the notion of Pareto optimality and the concept of social goods. The theory of inclusive finance finds its roots in the conventional economic theory of welfare economics. Second approach is based on the theory of finance centred around credit market failures. In addition to these traditional theories, the third approach is adopted by the recently evolving theories of microfinance discussing modalities and issues in operation of inclusive finance derived from the stylized facts. Recently, the theory of microfinance has been evolving from the stylized facts (Hulme, 2000; Fischer & Ghatak, 2011).

Economic Theories Providing Justification of Policy Intervention

The rationale for inclusive banking can be seen from the perspective of various strands of economic theory. As shown in Fig. 2.1, welfare economics and political economy are two of the main strands of economic theory addressing the need for policy intervention for providing finance to the poor. This chapter explores the welfare economics perspective. The political economy perspective is separately discussed in Chapter 5 of this book.

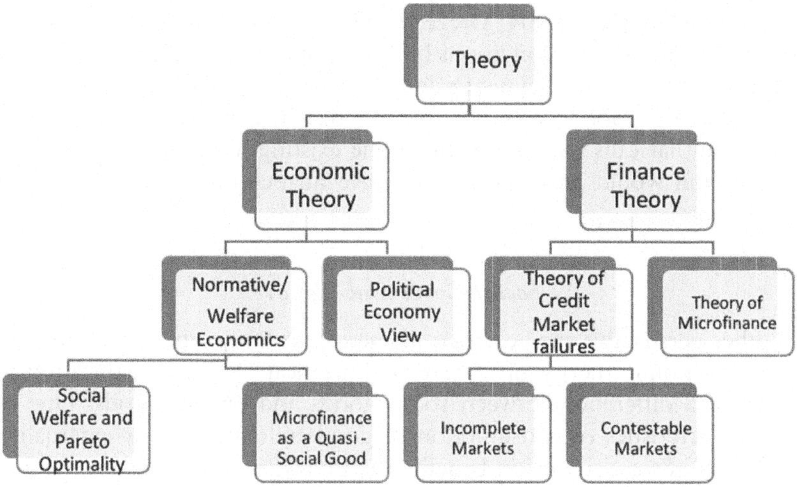

Fig. 2.1 Taxonomy of theoretical underpinnings of inclusive finance (*Source* Prepared by the authors)

Need for Inclusive Banking—Welfare Economics Perspective

The justification for why 'commercial' banks should be dabbling into inclusive finance to achieve 'social' objectives can be found in the theory of welfare economics.

Pareto Optimality v/s Maximum Social Advantage

Welfare economics rests on the premise of Pareto optimality and maximization of the social advantage. Pareto efficiency or Pareto optimality is used in economics to visualize a situation of maximum social welfare under the given conditions. This situation postulates such an efficient allocation of resources of the economy that it cannot be modified so as to make any one individual better off without making at least one individual worse off. 'Positive economics' postulates that the markets with their undeterred free market mechanism are capable of achieving Pareto optimality. This condition is criticized in welfare economics as it may lead to inequitable allocation and may not necessarily represent maximization of societal welfare (Sen, 2004; Dreze, 1987; Backhaus, 2005). Markets may lead to Pareto optimal conditions but may not achieve social welfare maximization. Hence, government's intervention is needed in certain cases. Financing the poor to achieve equitable distribution of resources is one such case that calls for intervention. The existing inequalities in resource distribution would never permit inclusive finance under Pareto efficient conditions.

Social Goods and Welfare

Another perspective the access to finance as an 'intangible good' or 'service'. Economic theory of welfare optimization provides justification in terms of a difference between social goods and private goods. One of the characteristics of consumption of goods relevant here is externality. Private goods consumption benefits the individual who consumes it and does not have any effect on the society. Social goods are those goods or services having externalities, i.e. their consumption or use creates benefits for the entire society. The market works efficiently in case of private goods as their demand reflects the amount individuals want to consume. But in the case of social goods the markets achieve a lower level of equilibrium as individuals are not concerned about benefit to the society. For example, education for an individual is beneficial with higher opportunity to get a job and earn higher income. In addition, the society is benefitted because when one more citizen is educated, it adds to national income, skilled labour force, better culture, lower crime rate and higher probability of next generation being educated. In private markets for education, not everyone may get educated because they do not afford to pay fees. If government intervenes and subsidizes education, then more people will get educated and the society as whole benefits.

In case of the financial inclusion, if the needy get access to finance, they can invest in microenterprise to earn income and improve living standards. The society will benefit from less poverty. But private credit markets cannot lend to the poor due to high risk and low repayment capacity. This provides a basis for the policy intervention in financial markets to achieve financial inclusion. The welfare economics theory supports policy intervention in cases of social goods having positive externalities for the society at large.

From a welfare economics view, government intervention is necessary to provide access to finance to the poor because access to finance has positive externalities. A poor individual getting reasonable access to credit and financial services leads to an increase in well-being of the family and in addition creates societal good by reducing poverty, reducing crime rate, etc.

Finance Theory of Credit Market Failures and Contestable Markets

Justification for government intervention in financial markets is provided in the theory of credit market failures. Since the private market mechanism is unable to arrive at an efficient equilibrium, the government's intervention is needed.

Positive economics view about credit markets, banks and financial intermediaries relies on free market mechanism guiding demand and supply of funds to achieve efficient allocation of credit in the economy. This problem of credit market failures is more aggravated in the case of credit for the poor.

Theory of Contestable Markets

The theory was advanced as a generalization of the theory of perfectly competitive markets and a generalization that (in contrast to the previous literature) endogenizes the determination of industry structure (Baumol et al., 1982).

The existence, or absence, of sunk costs and economies of scale are two significant determinants of contestability. According to the theory, asymmetric information proves to be the main barrier for the entry of new firms as incumbent firms have the advantage of knowing more about the market, demand and pricing than the new entrants. To safeguard this benefit and avert competition, the incumbent firms are reluctant to share their information with the new entrants.

The behaviour of banks in contestable markets is determined by the threat of entry and exit. Competition in the banking industry can be measured with the help of various indicators. For instance, analysis of interest rate spread shows that the bigger banks have it higher than the smaller banks, and level of spreads may indicate the level of concentration in the banking industry. The structure-conduct-performance paradigm examines the market concentration with the commonly used Herfindahl Hirschman Index (HHI). The contestability of the banking sector specific to a country is affected by the entry/exit barriers imposed by the regulatory framework in that country. Literature on new empirical industrial organization also provides some direct non-structural indicators of bank competition like Lerner Index, Persistence of Profits Panzar-Rosse Model, etc. (*Global Financial Development Report, 2016*. World Bank).

Overall, the entry and exit restrictions in the banking sector in developed countries are liberal and even the large banks are induced to act competitively. During the recent period after the global financial crisis in 2008, the competitive behaviour is curtailed by the regulatory policies and competition is reduced as indicated by the post-crisis Lerner Index or Boone Index values in the developed countries (*Global Financial Development Report, 2016*). Thus, according to the theory of contestable markets, government's intervention may be needed to manage the conduct of the firms that leads to monopolistic behaviour, price wars, high system costs and low social welfare.

A contestable market rests on three conditions:

1. Perfect information and access to the best productive technological know-how.
2. Free entry.
3. Free exit.

Without regulatory intervention, the banking sector is a contestable market as it has many players in the market, freedom to enter/exit and very low sunk costs. These characteristics can lead to highly contestable markets with fierce competition among the banks.[1] Thus, government regulation is necessary to curtail the adverse effects of contestability.

Theory of Credit Market Failure in Providing Finance to the Poor

The general problem of credit market failures is even more intensified in financing the poor and rural markets. A market failure occurs when a competitive market fails to bring about an efficient allocation of credit.

[1] The contestability of financial inclusion is discussed in Chapter 3.

In a credit market, the demand and supply of loanable funds are exchanged at a price, that is, interest rate. For the exchange to materialize, the price must be high enough for the suppliers and low enough for the consumers of credit. Credit markets are Pareto optimal when one cannot redistribute the credit to make one borrower better off without making another borrower worse off (Besley, 1994).

In the case of incomplete markets, however, the question arises whether the regular financial markets would work efficiently to perform the above standard functions of finance.

Constrained Pareto Efficiency in the Credit Markets and Incomplete Markets

Markets are not perfect, and even in a regular credit market, efficiency in the allocation of credit has to be examined in the light of these practical realities.

An ideal market where information is freely available does not exist. Credit markets in reality are incomplete with imperfect information for the existence of transaction costs. These problems result in a lower level of output and perhaps too much risk-taking. The Theory of Incomplete Markets argues that for subsidized credit the establishment of government-owned banks is essential due to the lack of constrained optimality.

The banks cannot afford to pay the high costs of credit underwriting and monitoring, and thus end up lending lesser amounts than required by each individual borrower. This situation cannot be compared with the theoretical Pareto efficient situation where the costs are assumed to be zero. This is a market failure. However, economists argue that a standard of efficiency impossible to achieve in the real world is not a useful test against which to define market failure. A Pareto efficient situation should be redefined to be applicable to the reality and outcomes like less lending due to monitoring difficulties are still efficient in a constrained sense (Besley, 1994; Dixit, 1987).

Thus, the Theory of Credit Market Failures proposes that the lack of inclusiveness in credit markets is due to deviations from the ideal conditions required for Pareto optimality. Although the credit markets are in themselves regarded as incomplete markets when the constrained Pareto optimality is not achieved, the situation calls for an intervention.

Credit markets and insurance sector are incomplete markets due to inherent features like imperfect information, public goods and externalities, and are existent in all the countries irrespective of the level of development. But in low-income countries, other important sectors like education, health care and rural credit exhibit severe features of incompleteness (Stiglitz, 1988, 1989).

Credit Market Failures in Developing Countries

The following sections discuss market failures as applicable in the context of credit markets and financial inclusion in developing countries like India.

Scarcity of Collateral Security

Lending in credit market is based on a bipartite contract secured by a collateral. The collateral security assumes a key place in this transaction of loanable funds as the transaction is inter-temporal. It implies that the lender provides the amount today but the borrower repays it at some future time. To guarantee the lender that the borrower will abide by the contract, a collateral asset is needed in formal markets. However, by definition, the poor lack the asset ownership and cannot provide a worthwhile collateral. Moreover, in the case of most of the developing countries, land or property cannot be pledged easily as land records and property rights are not correctly available in many cases. Thus, special policies are needed to include the poor and asset-less population in the credit markets.

Underdeveloped Complementary Institutions

Proper working of the credit markets requires well-informed participants, efficient channels of information dissemination, equitable socio-political justice, etc. Formal lending institutions like banks depend on legal collateral assets and so they cannot attain Pareto efficiency in case of lack of legal collateral assets. In developing countries like India, these institutional factors do not complement free competitive and fair credit market conditions. Poor borrowers have typically uncertain incomes, and hence, the risk of default increases. Insurance for income volatility is practically non-existent. This vulnerability of the poor population makes it difficult for the formal credit institutions in a free market to lend to those who are needy (Mendoza & Thelen, 2008). Thus, developing countries are fraught with deficiencies in complementary factors and institutions like transparent information systems, literacy, property records, bargaining power to fight legal battles for justice, etc. These deficiencies make the case for policy interventions in the credit markets. Since institutional changes and socio-political improvements are long-term factors, economic policy relies on active intervention to achieve the goal of access to credit in the short run.

Covariant Risks—Recent Pandemic a Live Example

Lending involves risk one of which is the risk of default when an individual will not repay the loan due to insufficient income. Covariant risk signifies the events with losses with high covariance across a large section of a community. Examples of events with covariant risk are floods, famines, epidemics, drastic global fluctuations in prices, wars, etc. The recent shock due to the pandemic and the loss of incomes of the poor, unorganized and migrant labourers across the nations is a case in point. This is distinct from individual risks, which randomly affect individual households. The recent pandemic is an example of the covariant risk where the entire economy is affected adversely due to the global disruption of economic activity. During this time, covariant risk is created by the uncertainty in income as the source of repayment of loan amount.

In the formal sector, the borrowers have secure incomes and the incomes of the individual borrowers do not fluctuate together in a normal situation. Borrowers of microlending institutions represent unorganized sector workers or rural labourers having highly fluctuating sources of earning.

In the case of unsecured incomes in the unorganized sectors, a single factor like the COVID-19 pandemic can affect the whole region. This covariant risk is reflected in the microfinance portfolios facing dwindling repayments and huge defaults due to the shock. In agrarian economies, this phenomenon is often observed due to weather fluctuations and results in large fluctuations in prices. Thus, a number of sellers of a commodity are adversely affected at the same time and this creates a possibility of credit defaults by many borrowers in that segment. This problem is accentuated in developing countries like India which have segmented markets. In these markets, a local moneylender has the benefits of low costs of information because he knows the history of the borrower and enforcement becomes easier due to proximity and community pressure.

But the covariant risk is high because local lending is availed by the local rural poor susceptible to income variations.

As stated by Mendoza and Thelen (2008), formal institutions like banks also face the risks due to segmentation of the market. The local lenders are better informed but the banks can mitigate the covariant risks by well-diversified portfolios across various segments.

Theory of Incomplete Markets

Credit markets are incomplete and characterized by a series of conditions, as described next, which prove to be barriers to achieve efficient equilibrium. These conditions are intensified in financing the poor.

Information Asymmetry & Microlending

Information asymmetry may be described with Akerlof's 'Lemon Problem' [1970]. Akerlof uses analogy of a car market to describe the problem in market mechanism due to information asymmetry. Lemon is used to describe cars in a poor condition. In a car market, the buyer has less information about the car quality than the seller of the second-hand car. As potential buyers are uncertain about the quality of the product offered, they would abstain from paying a high price for the product. Also, in such a case the seller would not agree to offer the product in hand at a price lower than its real value. A buyer facing the risk of buying the car asks for a discount in the price and such request might discourage the seller to sell. Hence, the flow of the market is impaired. Akerlof observed that in many markets these problems are not easily resolved, including insurance, labour and credit markets (Rosser, 2003).

Asymmetric information is a typical characteristic of credit markets. Asymmetric information implies that the lenders do not have accurate knowledge of the probability of default by the borrower, and hence, the lenders cannot price the credit accurately. The lenders have to incur high costs of underwriting or detecting the risky borrowers. They have also to incur costs of monitoring repayments. These costs are typically loaded to the interest charges and servicing fees (Hoff & Stiglitz, 1990). However, higher costs are regarded as unjust by the creditworthy borrowers and they are demotivated. Hence, this mechanism results in self-selection of risky borrowers on behalf of the bank and defeats the cause (Stiglitz & Weiss, 1981). Due to these problems, the lenders prefer not to lend in the markets where they incur high costs of information. The borrowers in these markets are typically thin-filed customers like informal sector workers, farmers, migrants and the poor. Thus, particularly for these sections of the population, credit markets with free market mechanism cannot sustain with asymmetric information and policy intervention is necessary to provide credit to these sections.

Adverse Selection, Moral Hazard & Microlending

Asymmetry in information in the credit markets leads to the problem of adverse selection. A creditor's lack of sufficient information on the borrower's risk rating and capability of repayment leads to adverse selection. Accordingly, borrowers with lower probability of repayment requesting for risky funds would lead off potential borrowers with higher probability of repayment requesting for less risky funds. A bank is not equipped with accurate information for each of the potential borrowers. Assuming the existence of borrowers with less probability of repayment, banks increase the interest rate and harden loan conditions. Paradoxically, borrowers with higher strength of repayment draw away from the market as they do not prefer such borrowing conditions. Therefore, the probability of granting a loan to an investor not eligible in a creditors' eye, namely the probability of adverse selection, rises. The same principle operates in the credit market for the poor as well and thus has to be monitored to ensure the access to credit for social advantage.

The banks also fear a moral hazard in lending in particular to the poorer sections of the society. Moral hazard implies giving wrong information to the lender in order to avail of the loan for the use other than that given to the lender. The borrower has an incentive to adopt riskier activities if these activities generate higher returns. Because the return to the borrower would be the portion of the project revenue remaining after the principal and interest paid. On the other hand, the creditor's return is the pre-defined interest irrespective of the project achievement. This results into a trade-off where the return to the borrower is directly related to the risk while the return to the lender is inversely related to the risk (Stiglitz, 1981). In the case of credit to the poor, moral hazard is common because of the borrowers taking up consumption activities or using the loan for the emergency expenditure without the approval of the bank. This is a common feature of microlending by banks. Hence, it is argued that the moneylenders are preferred as they cater to the peculiar needs of the poor and SHGs are better in loan monitoring. Thus, for a success in inclusive banking, banks have to heed these peculiarities.

Contracting Problems

The credit markets face contracting problems in providing credit to the poor and the unorganized sector. When a bank or financial institution provides loan, a contract for repayment is signed by the borrower. This applies to the lending to the poor also. However, problems arise in implementing and enforcement of the contracts in case of the poor, unorganized sector and rural sector. Enforcement is difficult in developing countries because of two issues as discussed at length by Stiglitz et al., in his *Theories of Rural Organization* (1994).

- Poor development of property rights in developing countries

  Generally, credit contracts are backed by collateral requirements. In developing countries, the ability of the lender institution to foreclose the contract in the case of default is too restricted. This is the crux of the non-performing assets problem in India. The foreclosure of loans by claiming the collateral is far from straightforward. Thus, the enforcement mechanism becomes toothless leading to more defaults. This situation in the case of regular loans is exacerbated for the economically backward classes and rural loans. For instance, on paper land is an ideal collateral. But in India the property rights to land are poorly drafted and recorded. Rights to land are based on use and transfer to others is complicated. Thus, for a lender, it becomes a lengthy procedure to realize the value of the land as collateral. Reclaiming assets through the courts is similarly not an easy procedure. This situation is also observed in other developing countries (Migot-Adholla et al., 1991).

  Studies show that in developing countries these problems lead banks to avoid this type of lending. This results in informal sector lending gaining a foothold as it can rely on social ties and community pressure rather than physical assets (Besley & Coate, 1991). Informal sanctions prove effective enforcement arrangements in the case of lending to the rural and poor people. For instance, defaulting borrowers in villages are not invited to the ceremonies. Land records and related legislation are key factors in rural credit markets where land ownership is the primary source of economic, social and political power (Attwood, 1990).

- Socio-political Complexities

  In developing countries, the enforcement of property rights becomes difficult due to socio-political conditions too. In the case of default, the lender is supposed to enforce the repayment but the cost of enforcement must be less than the benefit from it. In many cases, the lender may face non-monetary costs in addition to monetary costs. It is sometimes argued that rich farmers who fail to repay are not penalized because the political costs are too high (Beseley, 1994). In India, the debt waivering or loan waivering programmes where government announces that farmers would be freed from their past debts are frequent to the extent that at the time of borrowing, borrowers expect that eventually the loan would be waived if they do not repay on time. So borrowers are tempted to borrow excessively and defer the repayments. They regard loans as almost grants and thus have no incentive to use the funds wisely.

Less developed countries commonly face this situation leading to disparity of incomes and wealth, lack of opportunities and abject poverty, pushing their economies into low growth trap. These problems not only exclude the poor but at their worst they can make certain goods and services unavailable to them at any price.

Thus, it is important to identify these problems, providing solutions by restructuring markets and strengthening institutions, and then devising policy initiatives where the markets can work efficiently.

According to Stiglitz (1989), some market failures can be managed through non-market institutions through reforms in legislative and regulatory framework by the governments. Both the markets and the governments have their own strengths and weaknesses in resolving the problems and improving the well-being of the society. It is essential to identify these strengths and limitations for resolving the issues generated by market failures.

Conventional Economic Theory Stumped by Issues in Developing Countries & Stunned by Shocks

Economic theory of classical market mechanism believed that sanctity of the free markets need not be disturbed by government intervention to achieve economic growth. The first shock to this belief was the Keynesian Revolution. After the 2008 crisis, globally the role of the active intervention by governments is less stigmatized in economics. In India, the Andhra Pradesh crisis proved an eyewash for the veterans of free markets in the financial inclusion and microcredit arena. In the words of Ha Joon Chang (2011),[2] 'Following the outbreak of the global financial crisis of 2008, the state has made a dramatic comeback, after three decades of constant battering and vilification by the dominant neoliberal ideology'.

The recent pandemic crisis is seeing an encore for the state interventionist policy to revive the market for the survival of the poor. Thus, the traditional economic theory handicapped by its unrealistic assumptions and west-centric explanations neglects the realities of the incomplete markets and is not equipped to deal with the diverse socio-economic milieu and realities of the credit markets from the perspective of financial inclusion.

In this background, a third set of theories that exclusively conceives the credit markets in an imperfect socio-economic milieu and thus serves the microfinance agenda is worth paying attention.

Theories of Microfinance—Stylized Facts

The third set of theories is the newly evolving theories of microfinance that are derived not from the conventional economic theory but from the stylized facts presented by various empirical studies.

Fischer and Ghatak (2010) emphasize the need to bridge the chasm between the theory and practice in the field of microfinance. They argue, '…largely disjointed theoretical and empirical research in the area of microfinance has pushed our understanding to a level where the next great steps require unifying these two strands and the input of practitioners'.

Economic theory helps in conceptualizing the observations from empirical research. Empirical evidence is often specific to the underlying sample, while the theory helps in generalizing the findings to enhance

[2] https://www.redpepper.org.uk/the-revival-and-the-retreat-of-the-state/ June 7, 2011.

their applicability beyond the immediate context. Theorizing implies formalizing the relationship between variables and seeking predictability of that relationship. This is important for formulating policies. Theories can be verified with the data and can be revisited with the changing times. The field of microfinance has a plethora of empirical findings generated from the randomized trials and variety of other field survey techniques. Many of these findings challenge the traditional theories. Figure 2.2 provides a bird's eye view of the theories of microfinance. They deal with issues faced by the practitioners in microlending and financial inclusion. They are built around the issues and observations repeatedly evident across various countries and samples. Thus, they are stylized facts about microfinance.

These theories focus on joint liability, high frequency repayment and flexible instalments, and have attracted well-deserved attention (Fischer & Ghatak, 2010).

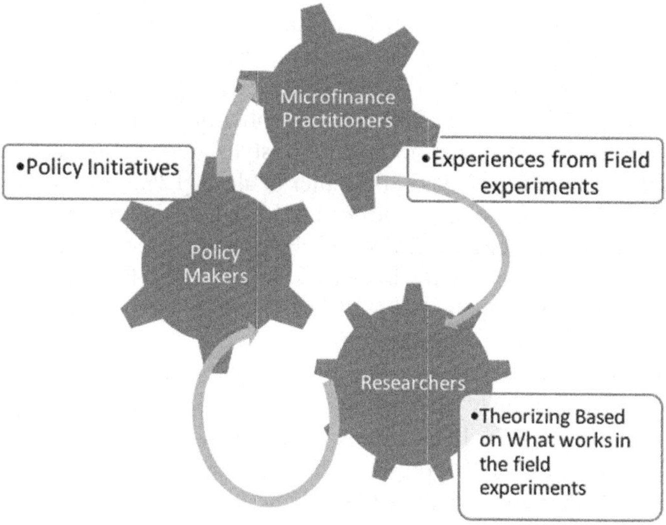

Fig. 2.2 Theory of microfinance—a melange of theory, practice and policy (*Source* Prepared by the authors)

The Stylized Facts for More Effective Relief Measures

Currently, the Indian government has declared moratorium for loan repayments including microfinance borrowings. According to theory, rational individuals should benefit from more flexible repayment schedules, and less frequent repayment should help reducing the default incidence. But actually more frequent repayments reduce defaults. So the importance of frequent repayment is 'theoretically puzzling'.

Fischer and Ghatak (2009) give an example of how stylized facts can change conventional theoretical beliefs. They give an example of an almost universal belief maintained by microfinance practitioners that frequent repayment schedules improve repayment rates. But the experience of practitioners and the emerging empirical evidence move beyond theoretical foundations.

The conventional economic theories are unable to provide an explanation for this phenomenon and so the policy initiatives that draw upon conventional theory prove unsuitable. Empirical studies show that behavioural factors like better response to imposed deadlines and tendency for procrastination are possible explanatory factors (Ariely & Wertenbroch, 2002). The 'present bias phenomenon' among microfinance borrowers is a well-documented stylized fact that explains the importance of frequent payments (Bauer et al., 2012). Empirical evidence on repayment frequency and reduced loan default is one of the stylized facts. Several studies empirically tested the positive effect of shorter repayment frequency on reducing loan default and their findings are mixed (Armendariz & Morduch, 2005; Westley, 2004; González Vega, 1998; McIntosh, 2008; Field & Pande, 2008).

Hence, stylized fact shows that reducing the frequency by allowing delayed repayment may backfire as the borrowers may not be able to bear the burden of the higher dues after the moratorium period. In the microfinance sector, more frequent payments reduce default.

Finally, Fischer and Ghatak (2011) may be quoted, '... in many cases, one genuinely does not know where to hang these results in our theoretical framework. Practitioners are pioneers whose work — both the successes and failures — gives researchers the basic material for thinking about what works and what does not work'.

Duflo (2005) beautifully captures this line of reasoning when she writes, 'Field experiments need theory, not only to derive testable implications, but to give general direction to what the interesting questions are'.

In the field of microfinance, the conventional wisdom of economic theories rarely applies. Hence, both the theory and empirical work have to be used to establish broad patterns or stylized facts. Ultimately, it is not of much importance whether the wisdom is grounded in theory or comes from an empirical field. What matters is whether it serves the policymakers and practitioners in their effort to reduce poverty and enhance economic growth.

References

Akerlof, G. (1970). The market for 'lemons': Quality uncertainty and the market mechanism. *Quarterly Journal of Economics, 84*(3), 488–500.

Ariely, D., & Wertenbroch, K. (2002). Procrastination, deadlines, and performance: Selfcontrol by precommitment. *Psychological Science, 13*(3), 219–224.

Armendariz de Aghion, B., & Morduch, J. (2005). *The economics of microfinance.* MIT Press.

Attwood, David A. (1990). Land registration in Africa: The impact on agricultural production. *World Development, 18*(May), 659–671.

Backhaus, J. G. (2005). *The Elgar companion to law and economics* (pp. 10–15). Edward Elgar.

Bagehot, W. (1873) *Lombard Street* (1962 Edition).

Banerjee, A. V., & Duflo, E. (2005). Growth theory through the lens of development economics. *Handbook of Economic Growth, 1,* 473–552.

Bauer, M, Chytilová, J., & Morduch, J. (2012). Behavioral foundations of microcredit: Experimental and survey evidence from rural India. *American Economic Review, 102*(2), 1118–1139.

Baumol, P., Panzar, J., & Willig, R. D. (1982). *Contestable markets and the theory of industry structure.* New York.

Beck, T., Demirgüç-Kunt, A., & Levine, R. (2009). *Financial institutions and markets across countries and over time: data and analysis* (World Bank Policy Research Working Paper No. 4943). Washington, DC: World Bank.

Beck, T., Levine, R., & Loayza, N. (2000). Finance and the sources of growth. *Journal of Financial Economics, 58,* 261–300.

Berger, A. N., & Udell, G. F. (1995). Relationship lending and lines of credit in small firm finance. *Journal of Business*, 351–381.

Besley, T. (1994). How do market failures justify interventions in rural credit markets? *The World Bank Research Observer, 9*(1), 27–47.

Besley, T., & Coate, S. (1991). Public provision of private goods and the redistribution of income. *The American Economic Review, 81*(4), 979–984.

Besley, T., & Coate, S. (1995). Group lending, repayment incentives and social collateral. *Journal of Development Economics, 46*(1), 1–18.

Chang, H. J. (2011). *The revival and the retreat of the state*. https://www.redpepper.org.uk/the-revival-and-the-retreat-of-the-state/ June 7, 2011.

Clarke, G., Xu, L. C., & Zou, H. (2003). *Finance and income inequality, test of alternative theories* (World Bank Policy Research Working Paper, #2984).

Demirgüç-Kunt, A., Klapper, L., & Singer, D. (2017). *Financial inclusion and inclusive growth: A review of recent empirical evidence*. The World Bank.

Demirgüç-Kunt, A., & Levine, R. (Eds.). (2004). *Financial structure and economic growth: A cross-country comparison of banks, markets, and development*. MIT Press.

Dixit, A. (1987). On Pareto-improving redistributions of aggregate economic gains. *Journal of Economic Theory, 41*(1), 133–153.

Drèze, J. (1987). *Essays on economic decisions under uncertainty* (pp. 358–36). Cambridge University Press.

Duflo, E (2005). Field experiments in development economics. In *Advances in economics and econometrics: Theory and applications: Ninth World Congress*. Cambridge University Press.

Field, E., & Pande, R. (2008). Repayment frequency and default in microfinance: Evidence from India. *Journal of the European Economic Association, 6*(2–3), 501–509.

Fischer, G., & Ghatak, M. (2009). *Repayment frequency and lending contracts with present-biased borrowers*. LSE Mimeograph.

Fischer, G., & Ghatak, M. (2010). *Repayment frequency in microfinance contracts with present-biased borrowers*. Retrieved from: http://eprints.lse.ac.uk/58184/.

Fischer, G., & Ghatak, M. (2011). Spanning the chasm: Uniting theory and empirics in microfinance research. In *The handbook of microfinance* (pp. 59–75).

Gangopadhyay, S., Ghatak, M., & Lensink, R. (2005). Joint liability lending and the peer selection effect. *Economic Journal, 115*(506), 1005–1015.

González Vega, C. (1998). *Microfinance: Broader achievements and new challenges*.

Greenwald, B., & Stiglitz, J. E. (1986). Externalities in economies with imperfect information and incomplete markets. *Quarterly Journal of Economics, 101*(May), 229–264.

Gurley, J. G., & Shaw, E. S. (1955). Financial aspects of Economic development. *American Economic Review, 45*, 515–538.

Guttman, J. M. (2008). Assortative matching, adverse selection and group lending. *Journal of Development Economics, 87*(1), 51–56.

Hoff, K., & Stiglitz, J. E. (1990). Introduction: Imperfect information and rural credit markets: Puzzles and policy perspectives. *The World Bank Economic Review, 4*(3), 235–250.

Hoff, K., Braverman, A., Stiglitz, J. E., & Ray, D. (1994). The economics of rural organization: Theory, practice, and policy. *Journal of Economic Literature, 32*(4), 1931–1932.

Hulme, D. (2000). Impact assessment methodologies for microfinance: Theory, experience and better practice. *World Development, 28*(1), 79–98.

King, R. G., & Levine, R. (1993). Finance and growth: Schumpeter might be right. *Quarterly Journal of Economics, 108,* 717–738.

Levine, R. (2005). Finance and growth: Theory and evidence. *Handbook of Economic Growth, 1,* 865–934.

Lucas, R. E. (1988). On the mechanics of economic development. *Journal of Monetary Economics, 22,* 3–42.

McIntosh, C. (2008). Estimating treatment effects from spatial policy experiments: an application to Ugandan microfinance. *The Review of Economics and Statistics, 90*(1), 15–28.

McKinnon, R. I. (1973). *Money and capital in economic development*. Brookings Institution.

Meier, G. M., & Seers, D. (1984). *Pioneers in development* (No. 9948, pp. 1–384). The World Bank.

Meier, G. M., Seers, D., & Bauer, P. T. (1984). *Pioneers in development: Second series*. Oxford University Press.

Mendoza, R. U., & Thelen, N. (2008). Innovations to make markets more inclusive for the poor. *Development Policy Review, 26*(4), 427–458.

Migot-Adholla, S., Hazell, P., Blarel, B., & Place, F. (1991). Indigenous land rights systems in sub-Saharan Africa: A constraint on productivity? *The World Bank Economic Review, 5*(1), 155–175.

Miller, M. H. (1998). Financial markets and economic growth. *Journal of Applied Corporate Finance, 11,* 8–14.

Petersen, M. A., & Rajan, R. G. (1994). The benefits of lending relationships: Evidence from small business data. *Journal of Finance, 49,* 3–37.

Robinson, J. (1952). The generalization of the general theory. In *The rate of interest and other essays*. Macmillan.

Rosser, J. B., Jr. (2003). A Nobel Prize for asymmetric information: The economic contributions of George Akerlof, Michael Spence and Joseph Stiglitz. *Review of Political Economy, 15*(1), 3–21.

Schumpeter, J. A. (1912). *Theorie der Wirtschaftlichen Entwicklung*. Dunker & Humblot [*The theory of economic development*, 1912, R. Opie, Trans.Harvard University Press, 1934].

Sen, A. (2004). Capabilities, lists, and public reason: Continuing the conversation. *Feminist Economics, 10*(3), 77–80.

Stiglitz, J. E. (1981). *Information and capital markets* (No. w0678). National Bureau of Economic Research.

Stiglitz, J. E. (1988). Economic organization, information, and development. *Handbook of development economics, 1*, 93–160.

Stiglitz, J. E. (1989). Markets, market failures, and development. *The American Economic Review, 79*(2), 197–203.

Stiglitz, J. E., & Weiss, A. (1981). Credit rationing in markets with imperfect information. *American Economic Review, 71,* 393–410.

Udry, C. (1990). Credit markets in Northern Nigeria: Credit as insurance in a rural economy. *The World Bank Economic Review, 4*(3), 251–269.

Westley, G. D. (2004). *A tale of four village banking programs: Best practices in Latin America*. Inter-American Development Bank.

World Bank. (2016). *Global financial development report, 2016*. Retrieved from https://www.worldbank.org/en/publication/gfdr/gfdr-2016/background/banking-competition.

CHAPTER 3

Inclusive Finance and Commercial Banks

The economic theories, policymakers and academics across the globe unanimously agree that the poor should be provided access to finance for alleviating their poverty. However, there is no consensus regarding how to devise specific policies to provide it. Questions which require deliberation are: (i) What should be the institutional mechanism for effective financial inclusion?; (ii) What are the pathways leading to financial inclusion?; and (iii) Is the commercial banking channel suitable for this purpose?

This chapter examines how the policy of inclusive finance in India strived to deal with the above questions. It provides an overview of the current status of microlending by commercial banks and the issues and challenges faced by banks in implementing the policy of financial inclusion to achieve the social goal of inclusion.

Although the definition of financial inclusion accepted by RBI visualizes a wide range of financial services ranging from micro-deposit mobilization to micro-insurance, providing access to banking services is the first step to initiate this broader process. Access to finance at the basic level implies access to savings and to borrowing through the ownership of a bank account. These financial activities are the basic operations to initiate the process of inclusion.

In India, Government's initiatives like PM Jan Dhan Yojana (PMJDY) facilitate these activities. To assess the success of PMJDY and any policy

L. Kulkarni and V. C. Joshi, *Inclusive Banking In India*,
https://doi.org/10.1007/978-981-33-6797-5_3

measures in general, it is necessary to define all pathways from the initiative to the end goal. In the language of experimental field surveys, using this mapping of pathways as a method for impact assessment is known as 'theory of change'. The use of the theory of change in this context is in a narrow sense only at the conceptual level and *not* in its true sense of application as an impact assessment method. Inclusive banking is a broad policy of banks adopting low-income group clientele as their primary customer base. We are using the theory of change principles and spirit to understand the pathways and preconditions to achieve financial inclusion through inclusive banking. Adopting this approach can give a clear visualization of both the challenges and the possible achievements of inclusive banking policy.

Theories of change link outcomes and activities to explain how the desired change is expected to come about (Clark & Anderson, 2004). A theory of change identifies the goals, preconditions, requirements, assumptions, interventions and indicators of a programme, providing important insight into and guidance on intervention and impact evaluation design (World Bank, *Theory of Change*).

Theory of Change: In the Context of Inclusive Banking

When we discuss whether commercial banks should be adopting inclusive banking, we use the theory of change approach to specify the pathways between the inclusive approach by banks and poverty reduction goal. This approach also makes one look at the assumptions upon which these linkages rest so that one could systematically evaluate the effectiveness of the bank channel. The theory uses backward mapping to create a set of connected outcomes known as the 'pathway of change'. The latter graphically represents the change process and acts as the skeleton around which the other elements of the theory are developed.

The theory of change is built in six steps (*The Centre for Theory of Change*, 2019):

1. Identify long-term goals: In the context of inclusive banking, the long-term goals are financial inclusion via ownership of bank accounts by the poor and poverty redressal.

2. Map backwards from the long term goals to interventions and connect the preconditions and requirements necessary to achieve the goals: The intervention in this case is the banks' outreach to the poor all over India and opening of bank accounts. The precondition in this case is that the poor have an know-your-customer (KYC) documents to open the account.
3. Identify basic assumptions about the context: The poor can use the accounts actively for their borrowing and depositing needs. Thus, once a person owns the bank account, it is assumed that he/she will be using it and will be included in the formal banking system.
4. Identify interventions that will create the desired change: In this case, the intervention is the provision of micro-accounts (PMJDY) with zero balance and other similar micro-lending facilities like Pradhan Mantri Mudra Yojana (PMMY).
5. Develop indicators to measure outcomes: In our case, they are (i) number of accounts, (ii) distribution of accounts across the country, and (iii) use of accounts.

Figure 3.1 maps the pathways from the policy initiative of PMJDY to financial inclusion.

In doing so, it specifies the outcomes that are measurable expected results in the medium term and also the assumptions on which the entire initiative rests. The assumptions are conditions necessary to achieve the outcomes and long-term goal. Thus, if these conditions are not met, then the programme would fail or would be only partially successful in achieving the goal. The programme would run into difficulty as other forms of lending like peer-to-peer lending are also coming in vogue and the big tech entry (through supplier credit or direct lending) could be a viable alternative.

Methods of Micro-Lending by Commercial Banks

The mechanisms used by commercial banks to provide microcredit differ across various countries. These mechanisms can be classified on the basis of various parameters. Conventionally, there are two methods of making decisions regarding lending: transactions lending and relationship lending.

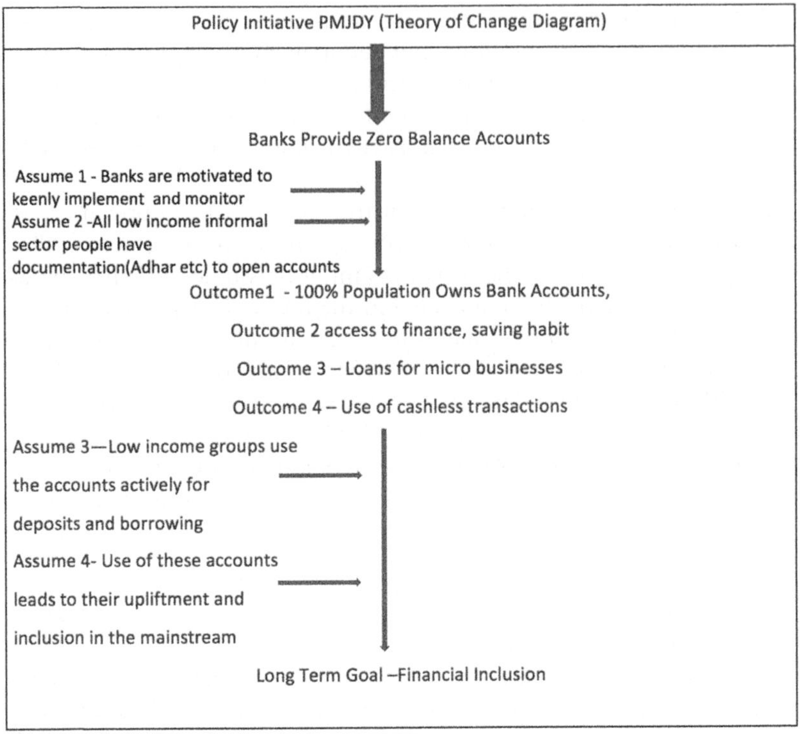

Fig. 3.1 Theory of change illustration (*Source* Prepared by the authors)

Transactions Lending: Commercial banks use financial data from the past years to screen loan applications. Mobile data of various sorts are now used to compute credit scores. These data include information on financial status, collateral, credit history, etc. This method is useful in case of the standard firms willing to borrow regularly. However, in case of lending to the poor and microenterprises, transactions lending is not useful as they do not have the creditworthy past records in almost all the cases.

Relationship Lending: Relationship lending is adopted when the lender knows the borrower well over a period of time. Thus, the need for risk assessment based on quantitative data is replaced by the use of qualitative information about the borrower. Moneylenders and MFIs adopt this approach. Institutions can adopt it in the case of MSME clients.

In the case of low-income retail borrowers, the usual credit market failures of asymmetric information, moral hazards become even more acute due to lack of collateral and inadequate trustworthy quantifiable data. In these cases, the lender avoids lending due to costs of credit monitoring as compared with the risk-weighted return and good borrowers are often devoid of loans (Stiglitz & Weiss, 1981). Digital lending will overcome these problems.

Relationship lending faces limitations in formal credit markets as the qualitative information is difficult to be transcribed in measurable parameters for a large number of borrowers. But the institutions lending to small borrowers find it more effective (Berger & Udell, 1995).

Comparative Advantages of Commercial Banks in Micro-Finance

Banks have an advantage over the alternative channels of microlending because their characteristics enable them to offer financial services to a large number of micro-finance clients without compromising on their profitability. In fact, they can be better microcredit lenders for the following reasons (Mas, 2009):

- Banks are well-regulated institutions. All rules and norms regarding ownership, financial disclosure and capital adequacy are well designed and monitored by the central banks to ensure prudent management.
- In India, public sector banks and most private sector banks have physical infrastructure including an extensive network of branches. Banks already have the operational structure in place to offer loans, process deposits and offer other financial products. As a result, it is easy for them to expand their customer base and reach out to a substantial number of local micro-finance clients through their branches.
- Banks have structured management that ensures internal controls as well as administrative and accounting systems that help them monitor large numbers of small-ticket transactions.
- In case of private sector banks, the ownership structure based on private capital encourages good governance, reduction in costs and financial profits.

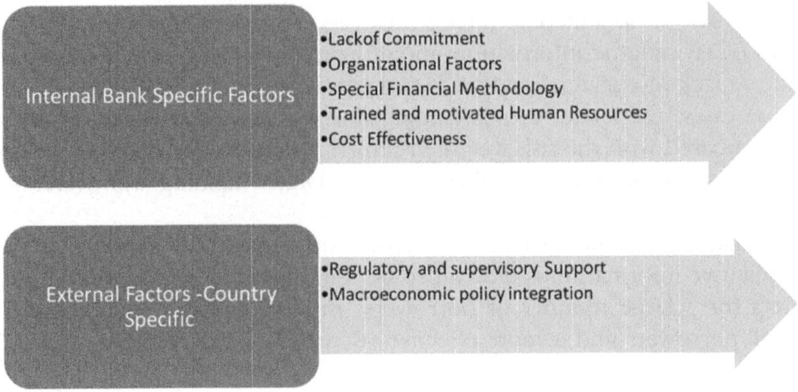

Fig. 3.2 Obstacles for commercial banks in microfinance (*Source* Prepared by the authors)

- NGOs have to source the funds from donor agencies while banks are financially independent because of capital and deposit funds.

Obstacles for Commercial Banks in Micro-finance

In spite of their comparative advantage, banks operate their microlending operations through MFIs or SHGs because they lack prerequisites necessary for expanding their customer base to low-income population. Figure 3.2 illustrates the complex mix of internal and external behavioural, operational and regulatory obstacles that commercial banks face.

Internal Bank Specific Factors Acting as Obstacles

1. **Lack of Commitment to Microfinance**: Across developing countries commercial banks are expected to play their role in microlending due to comparative advantages. However, their commitment to microlending is often inadequate. They treat microlending as a mandatory evil due to priority sector lending norms and other government initiatives. It is never their own child. This phenomenon is observed not only in India but across the globe. As stated in the Asian Development Bank working Paper

(Subhanji, 2016), the most crucial factor in successful implementation of microfinance by a bank is completely committed higher-level management. Only this can guarantee the necessary human and financial resources for expansion of microcredit activities by a bank.

In India, the public sector banks are expected to implement government schemes and loan waivers through their own resources. Across the globe, microcredit programmes by banks are funded through bank deposits without much dependence on donations and government grants. In some countries, small-sized banks are better committed to the microfinance portfolios due to closely knit ownership structures supporting well-oriented microfinance objective with well-designed products customized for the microfinance clientele. The business model of banks is discussed in Chapter 8. In India, the strategy of the banking business is never thought out on these lines.

In India, the public sector banks are under pressure to earn profits and compete with the private sector. The former are burdened with financing the government through statutory requirements. This additional pressure makes them less eager to pursue microfinance goals.

If the mainstream economic agents have a view that financial inclusion is an unwanted compulsion and a burden, then the policy will not be effective. Such provisional, ad hoc and shallow treatment will lead to more exclusion than inclusion. Real inclusion would mean making 'them' our 'own' to the extent that there remains no distinction. If the banks are convinced that the microfinance client base is not a burden on their resources but is a financially feasible business, then they will have the necessary commitment to achieve inclusion.

Organizational structure: Subhanji (2016) also emphasizes the importance of organizational structure, financial innovation and human resource involvement to achieve the cost-effectiveness essential for the sustainability of this business model. Organizational restructuring by banks requires integrating the microfinance programmes into their broader business model.

Adopting innovative technology and methods are essential to reduce costs and ensure risk management. Specialized human resource training is necessary along with special employee incentives for dedication to microcredit programmes.

External Factors—Country Specific

In addition to the above bank-specific factors, some important country-specific factors impinge on the performance of commercial banks as regards microlending.

Regulatory and supervisory support: Banks are subject to prudential norms specified by RBI as well as the Basel accord. These norms take into account the standard business of the banks assuming away the low-income clientele. The economics of microlending with a special risk profile requires that the regulatory and supervisory norms should be calibrated to the profile of the business with low-income clientele. Financial inclusion without taking into consideration low-income business clientele of banks is like an entity committing to open policy, welcoming differently-abled people in its premises but not bothering to provide ramps. The first step towards financial inclusion requires thoughtful reconsideration of the norms in tandem with low-income clientele and microlending business.

Macroeconomic policy: Including low-income population in financial landscape of a country is a long-run commitment that requires a paradigm shift in policy making.

Policy plays an important role in this. For instance, in a country like India with huge fiscal deficit, large domestic debt leads to financial repression. High cash reserve ratios and low interest rates lead to low profits for commercial banks, making it difficult for them to assume the risks of low-income client business. Thus, the perspective of the so-called mainstream economy should be to integrate the inclusiveness in the texture of the macroeconomic policy rather than providing exterior patchwork of inclusive policy initiatives.

Finding Way Through Obstacles—Strategies Used by Banks to Enter the Micro-Finance Space

According to the working paper by the Asian Development Bank (Subhanji, 2016), the main factors for the failure of commercial banks in microfinance are often the lack of adequate understanding of the microfinance market as well as high operating costs. These obstacles have been circumvented by some banks across the globe to develop this microfinance client base into a profitable business alternative. There are examples of banks that have found that the new microlending client base can be profitable business avenue. Banks can enter microfinance market through setting up microfinance units within them. They can also launch a separate microlending wing to cater to this market. Alternatively, they can refinance the microcredit of the MFIs and enter the microfinance market indirectly (Porteous & Isern, 2005; Sinswat & Subhanij, 2010; Bounouala & Rihane, 2014).

Direct Approach to Microfinance

1. **Downscaling**: When a bank enters the microfinance market by offering its services to the low-income clients and MSMEs, it is termed as downscaling (World Bank, 2013). This approach is used by nationalized banks in India to some extent to meet the priority sector lending targets. Since 2013, the banks are implementing the PMJDY and PMMY. Offering products like zero-balance accounts and microloans is in a sense downscaling.
2. **Business Correspondent**: Banks can appoint local agents to enter into microfinance market for mobilizing micro-deposits as well as for handling credit services and other payments, accounting services on a day-to-day basis. As these agents are locally situated channels, clients can have a comfortable communication and ease of access to them. They are encouraged to own and use bank accounts.

   This model is implemented in India by the commercial banks. In 2006 banks were given authorization by RBI to avail services of NGOs, MFIs, retired bank employees and ex-servicemen as business correspondents. This model aims at expanding financial services via branchless banking. In many places, this has been successful. The business correspondent model bridges the demand and supply gap (Subbarao, 2009) and is one of the most important initiatives that RBI has taken towards achieving financial inclusion.

   The model is a cost-effective measure to extend the outreach (Handoo, 2010; Dasgupta, 2009; Garg & Verma, 2016). Some studies suggested support from the banks with regard to increased commission, support for marketing, faster payment of commission and expansion of the range of products offered (Kapoor & Shivshankar, 2012). Some reports point out issues like dissatisfaction among the agents appointed due to non-recognition from banks and delayed payments/commission from the banks. In some areas, external factors like lack of basic infrastructure (high-speed Internet, frequent power cuts, etc.) created hurdles in effective service delivery. Studies report high attrition rate among the agents because of dissatisfaction among them due to non-payment or delayed commission from banks. Lack of support from banks also added to the misery of the agents (Jessica & Renuka, 2015).

From the bankers' perspective, the BC model also faces some difficulties. For instance, while BCs may demand to be absorbed into regular service, it is often difficult to waive all prerequisites and absorb BCs into the existing staff directly.

Banks use a BC model mainly to expand the coverage of no-frills account. Though the targeted number of accounts was met, in most cases they remained inactive or of low-usage (Chopra et al., 2012, Grameen Foundation, 2013).

Many studies suggest that post offices too could function as business correspondents (Damodaran, 2012; Singh et al., 2014).

3. **Internal Microfinance Unit**: A commercial bank serves small clients internally by setting up a separate unit that specializes in microfinance. This is not commonly done in India.
4. **Specialized Financial Institutions**: Banks can establish separate financial companies having a separate legal entity in the form of NBFC. This is not done in India although banks do finance MFI NBFCs.
5. **Microfinance Service Company**: Under this model, a bank establishes a separate entity like a special purpose vehicle. This does not come under the purview of the banking regulator. It handles the microfinance portfolio of the bank for a fee. The MFIs or firms having some experience in microfinance can provide this service to a bank for a fee.
6. **Equity participation by Banks in MFIs**: Banks can participate in MFIs working and provide them capital. IOB was requested to give Annapurna equity capital and in turn their two members were to be on its board, and monitor and supervise its working. This was in principle accepted.

Indirect Approach: Bank Partnership with Existing Microfinance Institutions

Outsourcing Retail Operations Through MFIs

As suggested by the study of Asian Development Bank (Subhanji, 2016), a bank can appoint an MFI with a record of a good performance to manage the microfinance portfolio (Fig. 3.3). This serves the purpose of achieving the benefits of banks as well as MFIs in micro-lending. In this model both the risk and profits are shared between the partnering bank and the MFI, thus maintaining a reasonable portfolio quality.

In this model, the bank and MFI decide which of them will make credit decisions or whether they will make joint decisions. The bank usually requires the MFI to partially finance its microcredit or guarantee a part of microcredit. This ensures that the MFI takes the responsibility of its microcredit, and reviews and monitors the portfolio. These loans are registered in a commercial bank's books. According to the regulations in different countries, often a bank may prevent an MFI from servicing other banks. With this arrangement, banks can benefit from MFIs' market knowledge, relation in lending and credit monitoring methodology. At the same time, the bank's funding and transaction processing capabilities make the lending efficient and well regulated. The advantage of this

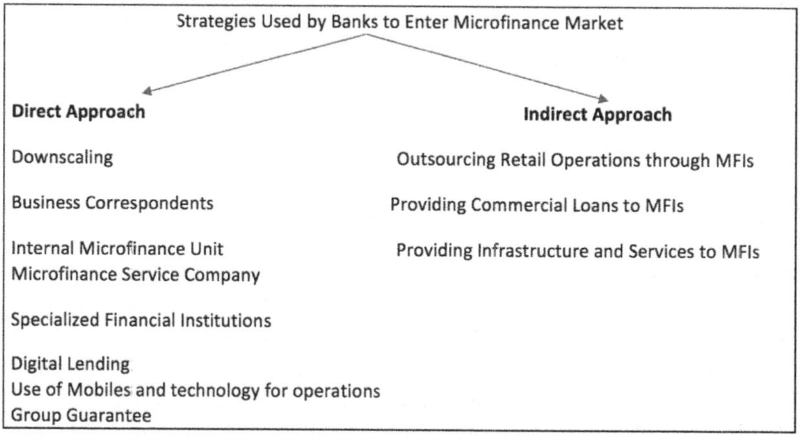

Fig. 3.3 Strategies used by banks to enter the microfinance marketspace (*Source* Prepared by the authors)

model is that the bank does not need to make a significant investment or operational changes in its regular business strategy to lend to small clients.

Banks can charge lower interest rate than MFIs: MFIs method of calculating interest is detrimental to the borrowers. Mostly a simple interest rate is charged and it is not reduced as the principal is repaid.

Providing Commercial Loans to MFIs

In this model, a bank lends to a microfinance institution on the standard terms of lending to a commercial unit. A bank in this case treats the borrower MFI as any other corporate unit and checks its financial statements, quality of management, credit history, asset quality, etc. It is, therefore, similar to normal commercial bank lending.

In this case, a bank provides credit to an MFI as working capital or to lend to micro-clients. Several banks in India choose this model of partnering with MFIs due to its simplicity, compared with the outsourcing model.

This model serves mainly the large regulated MFIs but the smaller MFIs may be side-lined in the regular credit underwriting process by a bank. This model is convenient for banks to lend indirectly to microfinance customers. The resilience of this model during the systemic shock events like the COVID-19 pandemic is questionable. Loans by MFIs become bad due to loss of earnings by the borrowers who are mainly from the unorganized sector. This adversely affected MFI loan portfolios and thus the bank loan portfolios.

Providing Infrastructure and Services to MFIs

In this model, a bank is least engaged in the micro-lending business of the MFIs. It provides its physical infrastructure and technological and personnel know-how to the MFI. It has the least exposure to micro-clients. This model benefits a bank as it receives fees and income in return from the MFI. A bank will also be able to learn the patterns, needs and behaviour of micro-clients from interaction with the clients of the MFIs. If a bank wants to develop this client base, it can benefit from it.

Subhanji (2016) reports cases of inclusive banking where banks have successfully collaborated with microfinance institutions. There can be internal microfinance unit established by banks, for example, in Mongolia and Turkey where the banks provide infrastructure, and easy, steady and low-cost access to funding and MFIs help lowering the operating expenses of microcredit. Another successful model of bank-MFI collaboration is microfinance service company where the bank establishes a microfinance service unit and undertakes its microcredit operations through it. This model is successfully working in the case of SOGEBANK with its Sogesol microfinance unit in Haiti. The third type of model is outsourcing the microfinance business to an independent microfinance institution where the bank is involved in funding, training and monitoring the MFI to provide low-cost customized products. This model is popular in India (e.g. ICICI Bank–Spandana) and has been implemented commonly.

Which Model to Implement?

Which of the above models will be appropriate for an economy depends on various factors like:

- **Country-specific economic factors**—The size of agrarian sector in an economy, the extent of unorganized/informal sector employment, risk and stability of the microfinance customer base, etc.
- **Country-specific socio-political factors**—Sociopolitical factors play an important role in the implementation of the model. For example, in developing countries SHGs linked to banks successfully work due to close community relations and peer pressure. Local political leaders also support and guide the groups in their areas.
- **Structure of the Banking system**—In countries like India, the banking system is well regulated and consists of state-owned banks. The financial inclusion drive and related-government programmes are implemented through these banks.
- **Systemic factors like COVID-19 pandemic**—The models are devised visualizing a 'normal' economic situation. They make the banks carry the burden of the entire microlending ecosystem. If and when a black swan event like the recent pandemic occurs, banks along with the entire system have a danger of collapsing and ultimately need to be bailed out by the government.

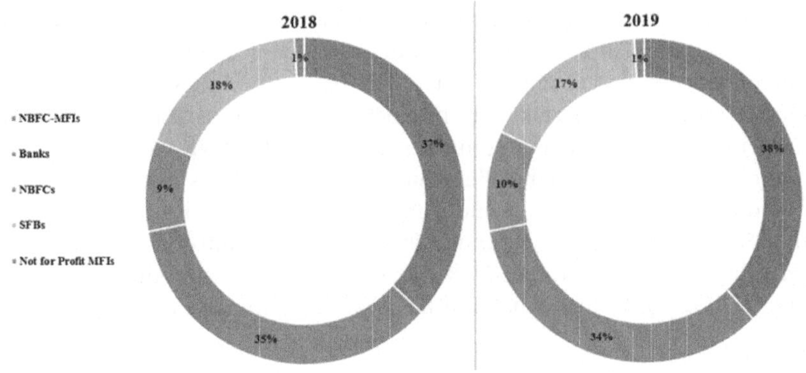

Fig. 3.4 Composition of microcredit by lender institutions (*Source* Bharat Microfinance Report, 2019, p. 68)

Current Status of Inclusive Banking

Though the official definitions of financial inclusion consider a broad range of financial services, most empirical studies use banking outreach as the key measure of financial inclusion (Sarma, 2008; Beck et al., 2009; Claessens, 2005; Gupte et al., 2012; Demirguc-Kunt et al., 2018). They specifically quantify the extent of financial inclusion using (i) number of branches per 1 00 000 population; (ii) number of ATMs per 1 00 000 population; and (iii) number of bank accounts per 1000 population.

The following sections examine the status of inclusive banking in India based on the above three criteria. Figure 3.4 shows the share of various institutional lenders in the microcredit.

The market share of commercial banks in the portfolio in microfinance industry is approximately 34–35% in the total market portfolio. The NBFC MFIs show 37–38% of the share. Nevertheless, they rely on the funding and refinancing by the commercial banks. This trend shows a clear mandate for bank-led financial inclusion in India.

Persisting Chasm Between Economically Developed and Developing Countries

Figures 3.5, 3.6, and 3.7 show the status of financial inclusion in select countries in terms of the above indicators. They show these measures

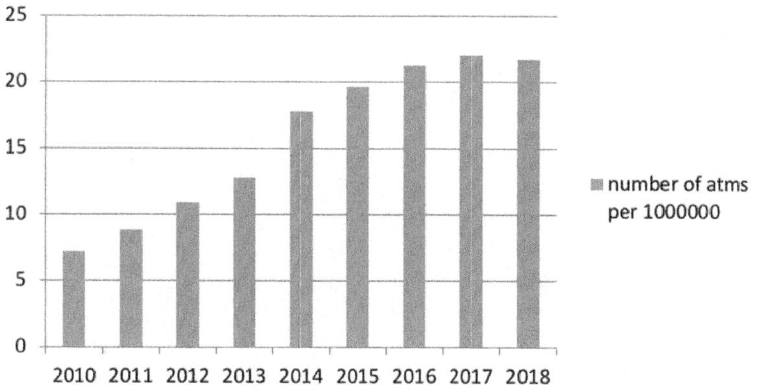

Fig. 3.5 Number of ATMs per 1,00,000 adults (*Source* Compiled by the authors based on Financial Access Survey, IMF)

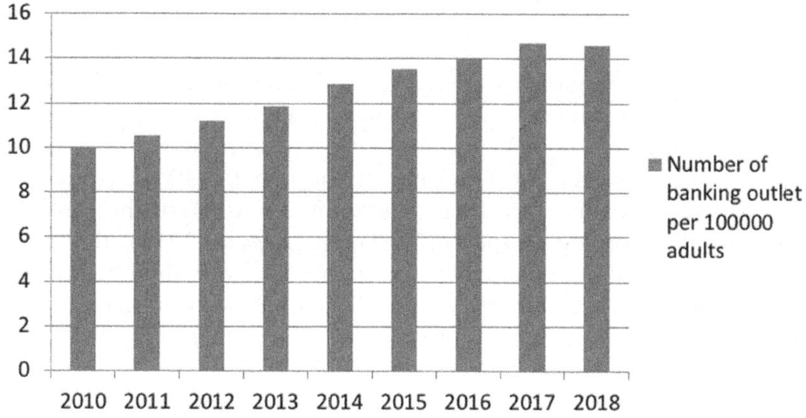

Fig. 3.6 Number of banking outlets per 1,00,000 adults (*Source* RBI, *Statistical Tables Related to Banks in India*)

across the country groups as per the IMF financial access survey data, and World Bank report, 2019. The data on percentage of adults with bank accounts is sourced from *The Global Findex Data, 2017*.

The data shows a wide gap between high-income and low-income country groups in case of the three indicators. India fares well as

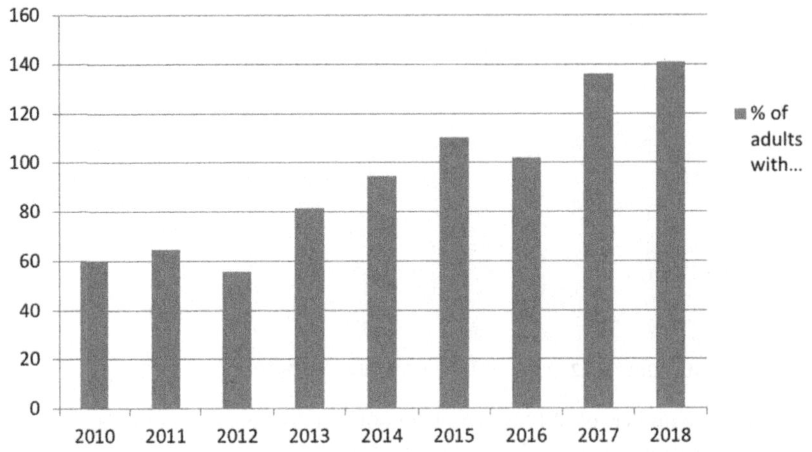

Fig. 3.7 Percentage of adults with savings account (*Source* RBI, *Statistical tables related to banks in India*)

compared with the global average except for the number of ATMs per 1 lakh adult population. The data shows a high percentage of adults with bank account ownership in India. This is attributed to the financial inclusion drive by the Government through the PMJDY initiative that aimed at opening zero balance accounts for 100% of the bankable population. According to the *Global Findex Report* (2017), the initiative was successful in opening of the accounts and increasing the number of account ownership. However, India is among the countries with the highest number of inactive accounts, with 27% of them reported to be inactive as per the *Global Findex Data, 2017* (Table 3.1).

Progress of Inclusive Banking Services in India

The progress of the outreach of banking services in India seems impressive if we have a look at the data on these three parameters from 2010 to 2018. This data from Reserve Bank of India shows that the financial inclusion parameters are consistently rising from 2010 to 2018 (the data for 2018 is for 9 months).

The trends in financial inclusion indicators in India show a steady and commendable increase. This is also appreciated by international organizations like the World Bank (*Global Findex Report, 2017*).

Table 3.1 Indicators of financial inclusion—global comparison

	ATMs/100000 adults	*Bank branches/1,00,000 adults*	*% of adults with account ownership*
High-income countries	68.14	20.3	92%
Low-income countries	4.07	3	33%
Lower middle-income countries	19.45	8.1	44%
Upper middle-income	53.97	14.8	61%
India	21.74	14.6	80%
World average	40.09	11.5	55%

Source Compiled by the authors from the *World Bank Report, 2019 The Global Findex Data, 2017*

However, if we have a closer look at the distributional factors, there are many issues camouflaged by this growth in numbers.

Deeper Distributional Issues Camouflaged by Growth in Numbers

Skewed Demographic Penetration: The progress of banking services in India shows that low ticket transactions have not increased in proportion. Hence, it is questionable how much of this increase has reached the bottom of the pyramid. The cost of low-ticket transactions has not reduced. Banking business in urban areas accounts for more than 75% of the total growth. The average amounts of the deposits and advances per account have also increased significantly, indicating that the increase in business is not due to the acquisition of additional customers at the bottom of the pyramid (Chakravarty, 2011).

Figures 3.8 and 3.9 show the number of banking outlets in villages and their growth rate from 2011 to 2018. The data shows that the growth rate is consistently falling throughout this period and even became negative in 2017–2018. This indicates that the growth of banking outlets per 1 lac adults shown in Fig. 3.8 is highly skewed in favour of the urban areas (Fig. 3.9).

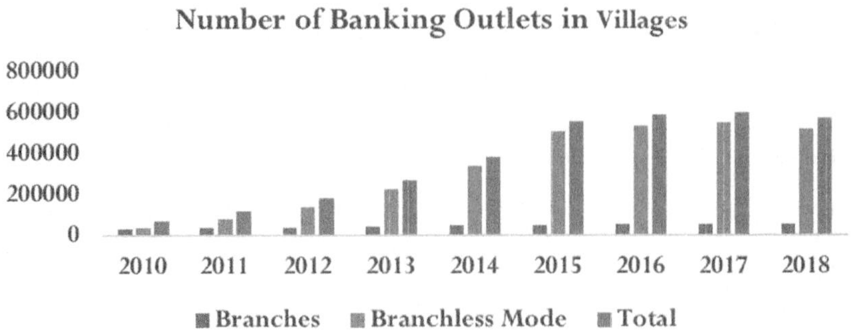

Fig. 3.8 Number of banking outlets in villages, 2011–2018 (*Source* RBI, *Statistical tables related to banks in India*)

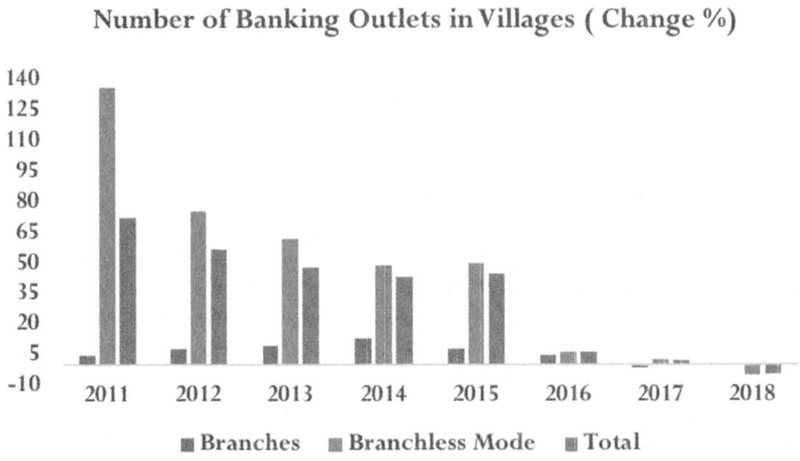

Fig. 3.9 Percentage change in number of banking outlets in villages, 2011–2018 (*Source* RBI, *Statistical Tables Related to Banks in India*)

State-Wise Data Reflecting a Regional Divide

In India, regional imbalances are evident in the financial inclusion parameters across the country. The three basic parameters showing the outreach of banking reveal that after fifty years of bank nationalization, the regional disparity in the outreach of banking services persists even today (Fig. 3.10).

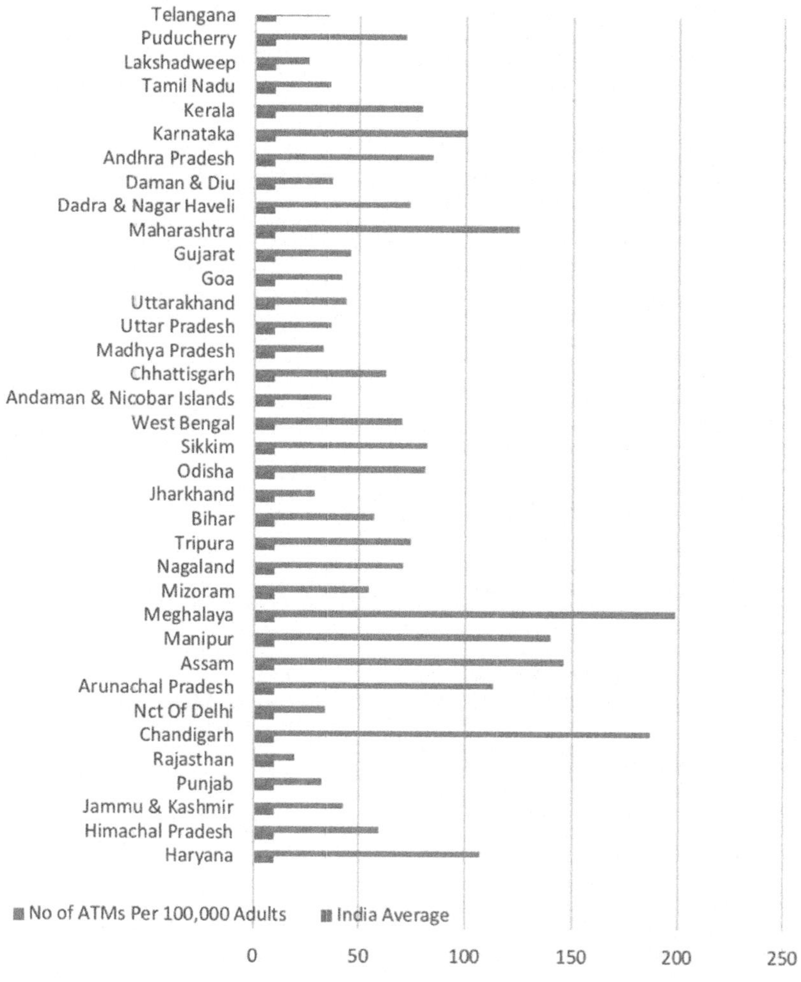

Fig. 3.10 State wise number of ATMs per 1,00,000 adults (*Source* Compiled by the authors based on World Bank data, 2019)

The ATMs per 1 lac population range from 19 per lakh population in Rajasthan to maximum 199/lakh population in Meghalaya (Fig. 3.11).

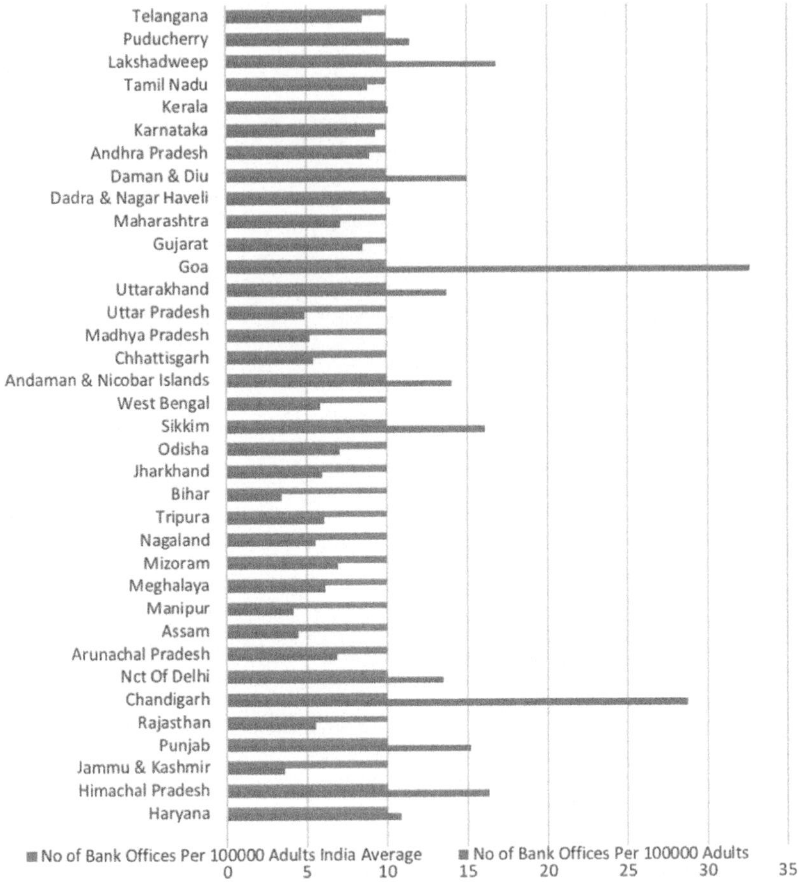

Fig. 3.11 State-wise number of bank offices per 1,00,000 adults (*Source* Compiled by the authors based on World Bank data, 2019)

The number of banking offices/lac population is highest in Goa at 33 per 1 Lac population and lowest in Bihar and Jammu & Kashmir at 10/lac population (Fig. 3.12).

The percentage of adults with saving bank accounts is highest in Chandigarh at 38% in India, closely followed by Goa at 37%, while the lowest in Nagaland at 7%.

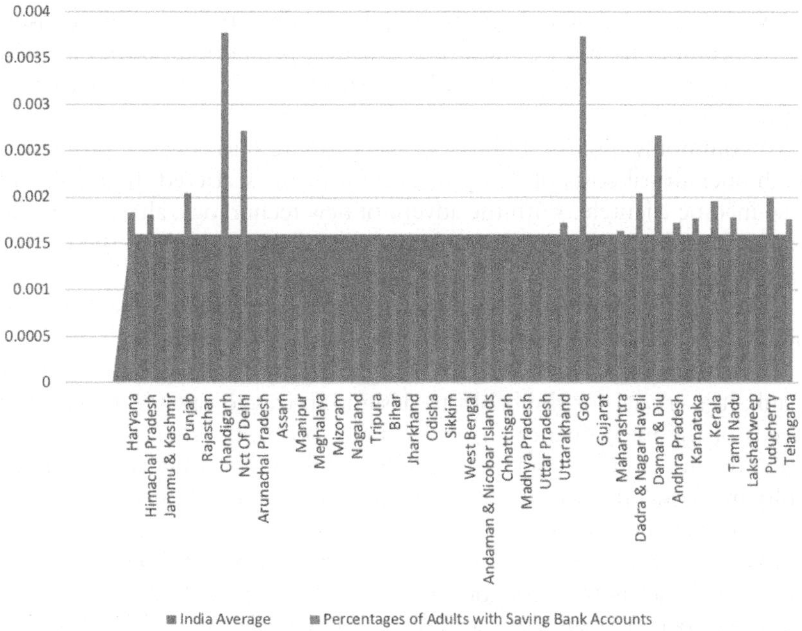

Fig. 3.12 State-wise percentage of adults with saving bank accounts (*Source* Compiled by authors, based on The Global Findex Data, 2017)

Key Variables for Successful Inclusive Banking

While inclusivity in banking is unanimously agreed upon in principle and is theoretically devised by various models, it is difficult to achieve it in practice due to various factors at play. These factors are case specific and vary from country to country and it is difficult to find a one-size-fits-all kind of solution. A common issue hampering inclusive banking is apathy on the part of banks to integrate microfinance into their business model because of their belief that this customer base is not profitable. Though they implement government-mandated inclusive banking initiatives, they view it as a burdensome duty than a potential source of profit. This leads to a high level of inactive accounts and skewed growth of banking in India. To tackle this problem, there has to be a paradigm shift in banks' approach towards this business. Public sector banks must recognize these activities as important and suitable weightage given to them while considering promotions and postings. For example, promotion policies in rural areas ought to be different than in urban areas, given the distinct needs of the clientele.

A commonly discussed hurdle in banks doing microfinance business is high operational costs of doing business with the scattered, high risk and low-income clientele. With the advent of new technology, alternatives like remote banking and mobile banking are available to reduce these costs (see Chapter 7).

The most common principles that can be adopted by the banks to achieve success in inclusive banking are summarized below.

Customized product design: As suggested by the Asian Development Bank, it is crucial for the banks to design services to cater to the specific needs of the microfinance clients who face problems when the products are difficult to understand. A microfinance client in particular faces difficulty in frequently visiting the bank and losing labour hours at the bank as commonly he/she is a daily wage earner.

Banks can diversify their risk with microfinance portfolio: The common belief is that portfolio risk in microcredit is low because of a large number of small loans and hence individual loan default does not affect the portfolio risk. Subhanji (2016) gives an example of Ag Bank in Mangolia that achieved profits through micro-lending portfolio even when the economy went through difficult times.

Change in perspective towards low-income customer base: In today's world characterized by volatility and global decoupling of markets, regular business of banks is affected by competition and instability from global shocks. Thus, banks must revise their business model to look for 'blue oceans' where the competition is less and profitability is more, but rather to focus on rural and low-income market segments (Chapter 8 discusses this model).

Using the appropriate Credit Mechanism: Small borrowers require different credit methodology than large borrowers. First, banks need to maintain regular contact with these customers for monitoring and recovery of loans. Borrowers must also be held responsible for intentional default. Banks such as ICICI Bank, Jammal Trust Bank and Sogebank use specialized credit collection mechanisms similar to those of the MFIs to succeed in microfinance (Subhanji, 2016).

Doing away with complicated processes: Complexity of banking products and delays in loan disbursements are regarded as demand-side obstacles to inclusive banking. In India, developing products that are easier to understand in a local language was identified as necessary by the microfinance customer.

Considering New Models: New models for inclusive banking can be explored, depending on the country-specific requirements. For instance, Sogebank in South Africa has appointed a service company for managing the microfinance portfolio. The bank benefits from the microlending specialization of the service provider while retaining its brand name and infrastructure advantage (Subhanji, 2016).

A different business model suitable for Indian environment is visualized in Chapter 8.

For the success of inclusive finance by commercial banks, the latter need to treat low-income segment as the core business rather than as an unwanted responsibility. Shocks like COVID-19 prove that microfinance institutions have their own limitations and the financial inclusion cannot successfully and effectively achieve its goals without a more dynamic and enthusiastic approach by the commercial banks. Global microfinance sector is in distress during the COVID-19 crisis. The crisis highlights the need for coordination between banks and local administration. Perhaps over a period such relationships will have to be strengthened.

References

Beck, T., Demirgüç-Kunt, A., & Honohan, P. (2009). Access to financial services: Measurement, impact, and policies. *The World Bank Research Observer, 24*(1), 119–145.

Berger, A. N., & Udell, G. F. (1995). Relationship lending and lines of credit in small firm finance. *Journal of Business*, 351–381.

Bounouala, R., & Rihane, C. (2014). Commercial banks in microfinance: entry strategies and keys of success. *Investment Management and Financial Innovations, 11*(1)(contin.), 146–156.

Chakrabarty, K. C. (2011, October 14). *Address at the FICCI (Federation of Indian Chambers of Commerce & Industry) – UNDP (The United Nations Development Programme Seminar on "Financial Inclusion: Partnership between Banks, MFIs and Communities"*, New Delhi.

Chopra, P., Narain, N., Pareek, A., Kumar, N., Bangari, S., Agrawal, S., … & Giri, A. (2012). *MicroSave Research*.

Claessens, S. (2005). *Access to financial services: A review of the issues and public policy objectives* (World Bank Policy Research Working Paper No. 3589).

Clark, H., & Anderson, A. A. (2004, November). Theories of change and logic models: Telling them apart. In *American Evaluation Association Conference*.

Damodaran, A. (2012). Financial inclusion: Issues and challenges. *AKGEC International Journal of Technology, 4*(2), 54–59.

Dasgupta, R. (2009, June 27–July 10). Two approaches to financial inclusion. *Economic and Political Weekly, 44*(26/27), 41–44.

Demirguc-Kunt, A., Klapper, L., Singer, D., Ansar, S., & Hess, J. (2018). *The Global Findex Database 2017: Measuring financial inclusion and the fintech revolution*. The World Bank.

Garg, P., & Verma, Y. (2016). Pradhan Mantri Jan Dhan Yojana (PMJDY): A step towards eradicating financial untouchability. *Indian Journal of Finance, 10*(1), 56–64. https://doi.org/10.17010/ijf/2016/v10i1/85845.

Grameen Foundation. (2013). *Addressing dormancy in savings accounts: Insights from the Cashpor BC project* (1–14). http://www.grameenfoundation.in/wpcontent/uploads/2013/07/Addressing-Dormancy-Insights-from-the-GFI-Cashpor-BCProject.pdf.

Gupte, R., Venkataramani, B., & Gupta, D. (2012). Computation of financial inclusion index for India. *Procedia-Social and Behavioral Sciences, 37*, 133–149.

Handoo, J. (2010). *Financial inclusion in India: Integration of technology, policy and market at bottom of the pyramid*. Available at: http://ssrn.com/abstract¼1628564.

IMF Financial Access Survey dataset. https://data.imf.org/?sk=E5DCAB7E-A5CA-4892-A6EA-598B5463A34C&sId=1393552803658.

Jessica, V., & Renuka, B. (2015). BC model of financial inclusion through business correspondent's perspective DAWN. *Journal for Contemporary Research in Management, 2*(1), 27–34.

Kapoor, R., & Shivshankar, V. (2012). *State of business correspondent Industry in India–The supply side story*.

Mas, I. (2009). The economics of branchless banking. *Innovations: Technology, Governance, Globalization, 4*(2), 57–75.

Mas, I., Tiwari, A., Jos, A., George, D., Thacker, K. U. M., Garg, N., ... & Shukla, V. (2012). *Are banks and microfinance institutions natural partners in financial inclusion?*

Oxford University Press, The World Bank Research Observer Advance Access (2009).

Porteous, D., & Isern, J. (2005). Commercial banks and microfinance: evolving models of success. *Focus Note, 28*.

RBI. Database on Indian Economy.

Sarma, M. (2008). *Index of financial inclusion* (Working paper 215). Indian Council for Research on International Economic Relations.

Singh, C., et al. (2014). Financial inclusion in India: Select issues. *IIMB Working Paper* (474), 1–43. Retrieved from https://www.iimb.ernet.in/research/sites/default/files/WPNo.474.pdf.

Sinswat, W., & Subhanij, T. (2010). *A cross-country survey on SME financial access and implications for Thailand* (No. 2010-03).

Stiglitz, J. E., & Weiss, A. (1981). Credit rationing in markets with imperfect information. *American Economic Review, 71,* 393–410.

Subbarao, D. (2009). *Remarks at the Bankers' Club in Kolkata on December 9, 2009*. https://rbidocs.rbi.org.in/rdocs/Speeches/PDFs/IFFG091209.pdf.

Subhanij, T. (2016). *Commercial bank innovations in small and medium-sized enterprise finance: Global models and implications for Thailand* (ADBI Working Paper 583). Tokyo: Asian Development Bank Institute. Available: http://www.adb.org/publications/commercialbank-innovations-sme-finance-global-models-implications-thailand/.

The Centre for Theory of Change. (2019). *How does theory of change work?* http://www.theoryofchange.org/what-is-theory-of-change/how-does-theory-of-change-work/.

Theory of Change Online (TOCO) Community. *Theory of change and logic models*. http://www.theoryofchange.org/wp-content/uploads/toco_library/pdf/TOCs_and_Logic_Models_forAEA.pdf.

The World Bank. *Theory of change*. https://dimewiki.worldbank.org/wiki/Theory_of_Change.

CHAPTER 4

The Non-Bank Sources of MicroLending in India

In the formal microfinance sector, microlending and deposit providers can be classified into banks and non-bank institutions. The non-bank side of the Indian microfinance sector consists of many formal, semi-formal and informal players. All of these participants in the micro-lending market are co-dependent, forming a complex network. The current chapter discusses the most popular formal sector sources of microcredit in India, namely, microfinance institutions (NBFC–MFIs) and Self-Help Groups (SHGs).

The informal microfinance sector survives and thrives because of the gaps between the needs of small borrowers and services offered by the formal micro-lending institutions. If these gaps were bridged by the formal sector, then the incidence of informal sector would be automatically reduced. It is, therefore, necessary to identify these gaps and discuss the issues faced by the formal sector microfinance institutions. As discussed earlier, the special nature of market failures calls for relationship lending to achieve successful and sustainable microfinance. As a result of these market failures, the non-bank financial intermediaries are more efficient in lending to the poor. The network approach to microfinance shows that the ecosystem of non-bank MFIs and SHGs is ultimately dependent on the banks for refinancing. This codependency of MFIs and banks has become all the more evident during the circumstances created by the COVID-19 pandemic.

L. Kulkarni and V. C. Joshi, *Inclusive Banking In India*,
https://doi.org/10.1007/978-981-33-6797-5_4

This chapter focuses on the issues of NBFC MFIs, link between these non-bank sources of micro credit with the banks, their codependency on each other and the current problems in the NBFC sector acting as hurdles for achieving financial inclusion.

Taxonomy of Non-Bank Micro Finance Institutions in Formal Microfinance Sector

By definition, banks are deposit taking financial intermediaries. Non-bank financial intermediaries by definition do not mobilize deposits in the sense that they do not create credit based on a fractional reserve system (i.e. the normal conventional banking of lending and borrowing). The non-bank financial sector consists of a vast and diverse universe of the non-bank financial corporations (NBFCs), NBFC–MFIs, U/S 8 companies, societies, trusts, cooperatives, etc. Out of these entities, NBFC–MFIs are 'For Profit' microlending institutions in the formal segment of the NBFCs.

In addition to MFIs, there are co-operative societies, MFI-banks, SHGs, Joint Liability Groups, etc. This microfinance landscape in India is shown in Fig. 4.1.

The following sections provide an overview of these institutions and discuss the challenges faced by them.

Development of Microfinance NBFCs in India

The developments in India's microfinance sector can be categorized into three stages: (i) the pre-Andhra Pradesh crisis period (prior to 2010), (ii) post-Andhra Pradesh crisis period (from 2010 to 2020), and (iii) period after the pandemic crisis (post-2020).

The Pre-Andhra Pradesh Crisis Period

The origin of the Indian MFIs can be traced back to humble beginnings made by Prof. Kavatheker at Baroda in 1905 who formed Anyonya Sahakari Society. He formed a small self-help group that helped members in need of financial help. Small loans were made by it and the timely help gave respite to the members to tide over their immediate problems. The group activities were modelled on the lines of German agrarian models prevalent in the 1880s. One could consider this as the beginning of the early group micro-lending activities in India in the formal sector.

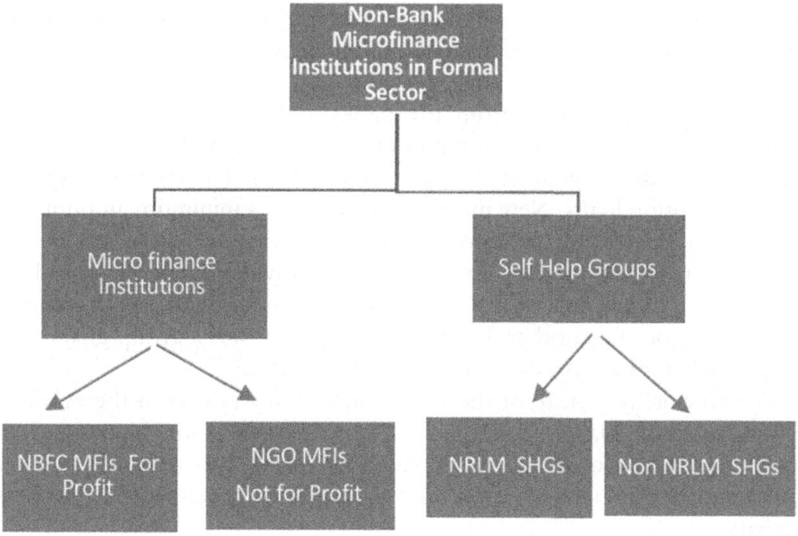

Fig. 4.1 Taxonomy of non-bank microfinance institutions in formal sector (*Source* Compiled by the authors)

In India, there are many instances of the microfinance activities undertaken initially in the form of voluntary activities to help the needy on a small scale and which later evolved into a large institutional set up. For example, SEWA (Self-Employed Women's Association). It grew out of the Textile Labour Association (TLA), India's oldest and largest union of textile workers founded in 1920 by Anasuya Sarabhai and Prema Purao in Maharashtra and which initiated microfinance activities at local level. Both of them worked with the mill workers and bank employees' unions and tried to relieve the wives of the workers from the clutches of the moneylenders. In 1971, Ela Bhatt, and Arvind Buch, launched SEWA—the Self-Employed Women's Association. Mrs. Purao of Annapurna started with borrowing from the nationalized banks under the differential interest rates (DIRs) scheme for lending to the millworkers' wives. They would then send out lunch baskets to the workers belonging to the given village. This became a supplementary source of income and, thanks to the organization to which they belonged, they could buy grains and provisions from the wholesale market. Gradually Annapurna founded by Mrs. Purao, became a full-fledged MFI while SEWA founded by Mrs.

Bhat became the largest organization of informal workers in the world and largest non-profit organization in India. Many of the microfinance institutions in India have a similar trajectory.

They borrowed funds from the banks at cheaper rates. They were lent to the members both for consumption loans and occasionally for meeting working capital needs. The primary focus had over time shifted to consumption loans. New members were given a minimum amount and became eligible for higher amounts over the course of 12–15 months.

The loans were used by the concerned individuals but the members had to be attached to a group of five other members who would stand as guarantors for one another. In other words, there was a group guarantee. Similar schemes are prevalent in Bangladesh today.

A noteworthy feature of the whole operation was that in the event of failure, even on a large scale, the bank was responsible for the money lost in the lending operation. The profit, however, went to the MFI. What started originally as a salvation army help group turned into a business activity.

The whole activity suffers from certain weaknesses as enumerated below.

Under the liberal dispensation, it was believed that given the monetary support, members of the groups would become entrepreneurs. This assumption has not quite worked out. Most of those who borrowed the funds did so to meet consumption needs and to pay medical or school fees. Secondly (and this was a fundamental weakness), as evidenced by several surveys (Banerjee & Duflo, 2011), most members looked for gainful employment in either factories or offices.

The group guarantee scheme also leaves much to be desired. The recovery process was torturous and many members suffered. Repayment instalments were not based on the members' capacity to pay. It even led to the unhealthy practice of intra-group lending. No doubt this system was better than that of borrowing directly from the moneylenders but was not conducive to development. Evaluation exercises by Duflo and Banerjee (2011) revealed this glaring drawback.

Not all MFIs were oriented towards members' welfare but operated like a profit-seeking enterprise. Activities like increasing members' income or improving children's education and health were of little interest to them. A study by Joshi et al. (2012) for the Council of World Affairs shows how the reality differed and the myth persisted. The mission statement and actual working of some of these organizations showed variance. Therefore, Andhra Crisis was inevitable.

Post- Andhra Pradesh Crisis MFI Sector

The Andhra Pradesh crisis led to a paradigm shift in regulation, structure, and conduct of the entire MFI sector. In its wake, under the chairmanship of Y H Malegam the Reserve Bank constituted a committee to study the microfinance sector. In December 2011, based on its report, a separate category of NBFC–MFIs was created along with a regulatory framework. Additionally, they came under section 25 of the Companies' Act, 1956. It controlled the registration, licensing and capital adequacy of the MFIs, thereby pruning their rampant growth. However, the interest charged and the recovery mechanisms are still non-relenting. The growth of NBFC MFIs is depicted in Figs. 4.2, 4.3, and 4.4.

Thus, the growth of MFIs in India was rampant and unregulated until 2011. After 2012, the number of MFIs decreased, as the RBI implemented regulation.

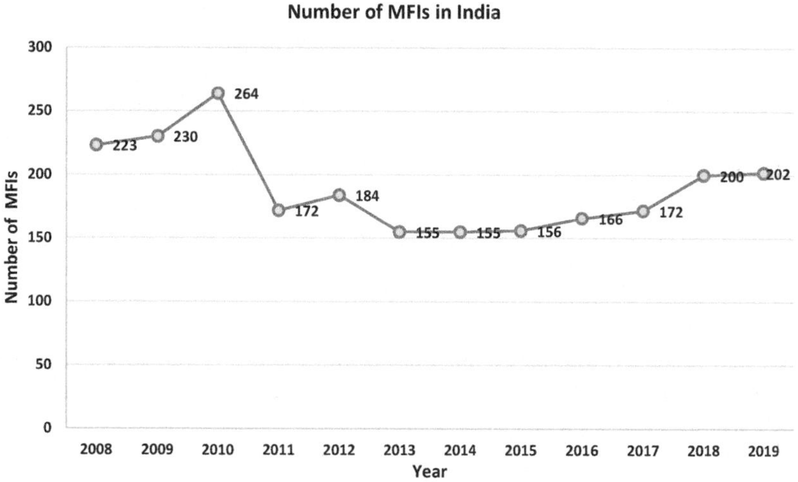

Fig. 4.2 Growth in number of MFIs in India (*Source: Bharat Microfinance Report, 2008–2010*)

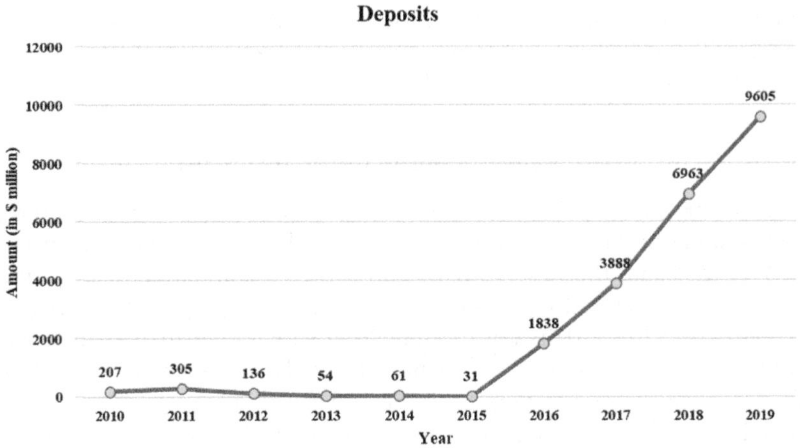

Fig. 4.3 Deposits in microfinance institutions in India (*Source* Based on MIX Market, Database, The World Bank, www.databank.worldbank.org)

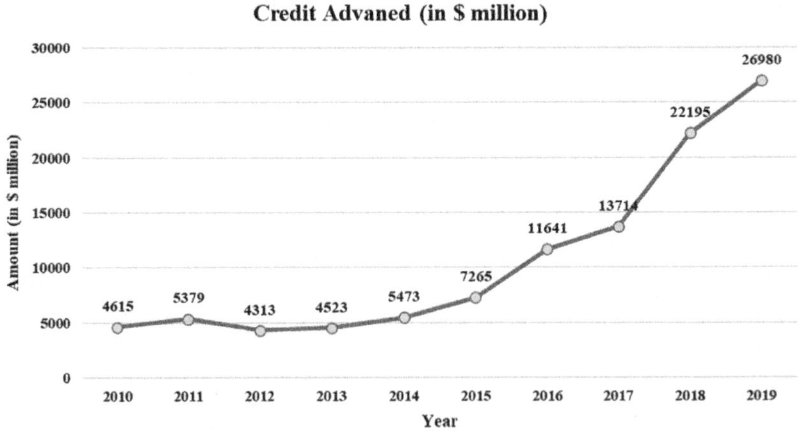

Fig. 4.4 Credit Advanced by Microfinance Institutions in India (*Source* Based on MIX Market, Database, The World Bank, www.databank.worldbank.org)

The growth in deposits of and credit by the NBFC MFIs since 2010 is seemingly impressive and the Indian MFI sector may be regarded as one of the largest microfinance sectors in the world. Figures 4.3 and 4.4 show high growth in the NBFC MFI sector. However, this growth in numbers camouflages those evolving trends that can be self-defeating.

Stunted Growth of not for Profit MFIs (NGO-MFIs)

The microfinance sector also consists of not-for-profit NGO-MFIs. In fact, the first generation of microfinance institutions was not for profit MFIs established by the NGOs like MYRADA, SEWA and Annapurna. Today, however, the growth of not-for-profit NGO-MFIs is stunted and for-profit MFIs are more prominent in the NBFC–MFI sector. Many of the non-profit institutions have begun providing day-care centres, primary education or training in reading and numerical skills to sustain the competition.

The risk profile of the microfinance sector also reflects its imbalanced structure. Figure 4.5 shows the portfolio risk in terms of loan delinquency

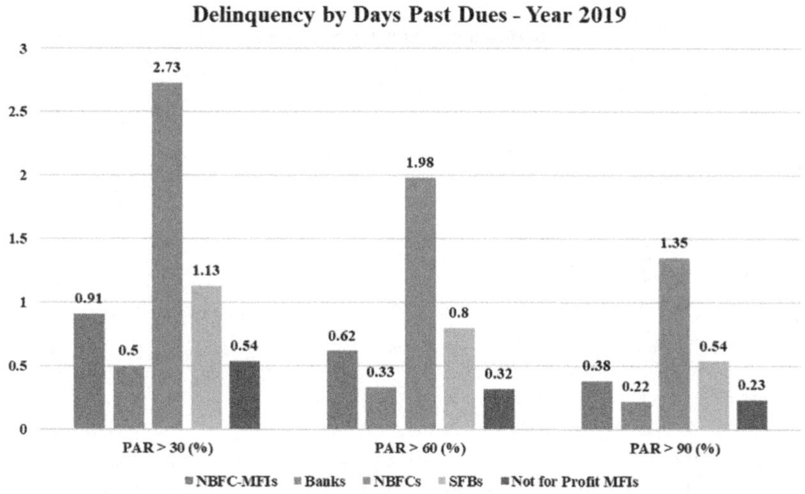

Fig. 4.5 Delinquency by days past dues (*Source Bharat Microfinance Report, 2019*, p. 70)

in terms of number of days due. The riskyness of NBFCs is the highest, followed by that of the small finance banks and NBFC MFIs.

As seen in Fig. 4.6, the NBFC–MFI sector has more borrowers and higher lending as compared to banks, SFBs, NBFCs and not-for-profit MFIs. Despite the fact that the microfinance movement stands on the foundation laid by NGOs, at present the proportion of NGO MFIs in the total microfinance landscape is alarmingly small.

The NBFC–MFI average ticket size is lower than all the other microlending providers in the sector. This shows a better outreach to the microcredit customers. In terms of 30+ days and 90+ days delinquency, the NBFC MFI sector fares better than the small finance banks and NBFCs. MFIs hold the largest share of the loan portfolio which stands at INR 681 billion accounting for 38% of the total industry portfolio (*Microfinance Pulse Report, SIDBI & Equifax, 2019*). This suggests that borrowers are more inclined to take loans from MFIs.

According to the reports of June 2020, NBFC MFIs show some decrease due to the impact of COVID-19. Earlier the gross loan portfolio had registered a growth of 31% to Rs 74,371 crore at the end of March 2020, according to MFIN. The portfolio stood at Rs 56,683 crore in 2018–2019.

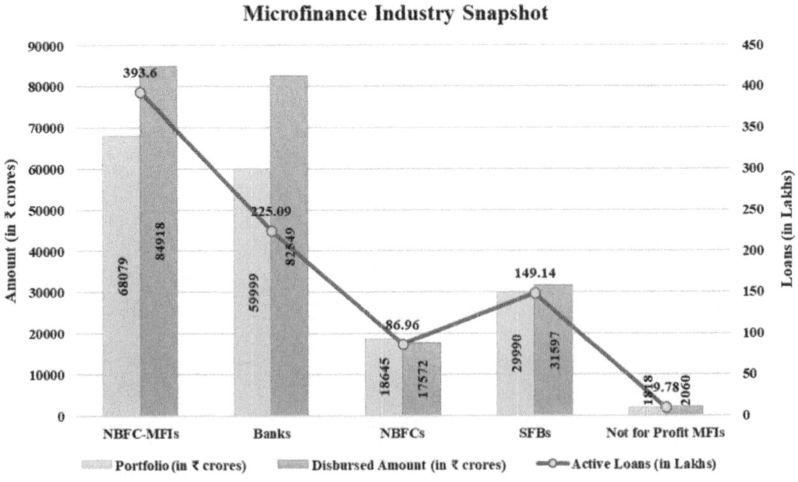

Fig. 4.6 Loan portfolios-microfinance industry snapshot (*Source Bharat Microfinance Report, 2019*, pp. 66, 68 & 75)

Average loan amount disbursed per account during 2019–2020 was Rs 27,754, which is an increase of around 6% in comparison with loans disbursed during 2018–2019 (*MFIN's Micrometre report* for January–March 2020).

Interestingly, the commercial banks hold the largest share (39.8%) in the total loans outstanding in microcredit portfolio, followed by NBFC–MFIs at 31.8%.

In terms of loan disbursement, the top-10 MFIs accounted for 70% of overall industry disbursements. Duflo and Banerjee (2011), however, have shown that the resultant impacts on education, health and income were marginal.

Overview of SHGs Linked to Banks

Evolution: The policy initiative to institutionalize the SHG movement in India was taken by the National Bank for Rural Development (NABARD) in the early 1980s. Prior policy of financial inclusion focused on the credit side. NABARD emphasized that the poor-needed savings schemes designed to cater to their needs. As reported by Seibel (2012), this initiative to institutionalize the SHGs was based on motivation from a Asia-specific regional level initiative of *Linking Banks and Self-help Groups* undertaken by APRACA and GTZ/GIZ in Asia. NABARD initiated a study of SHGs in 1987, led by MYRADA and based on the new paradigm of *savings first*.

SHG Bank-linked programme is a commendable effort to link the SHGs from the informal sector to the banks and microfinance institutions in the formal sector. NABARD, through the department of 'Micro Credit Innovations', has continued its role as the facilitator of microfinance initiatives. The programme, started during 1992–1993, has become the largest microfinance programme in the world in terms of the client base and outreach (Seibel, 2012).

The programme visualized an elaborate conglomerate of institutions as facilitators, organizers and enablers of linkage between the SHGs and banks. These self-help promoting institutions (SHPIs) are NGOs as well as rural financial institutions (RRBs, DCCBs, PACS, Farmers' Clubs (FCs), SHG Federations, NGO-MFIs, Individual Rural Volunteers (IRVs), etc.).

These SHPIs take up promotion of SHGs by way of promotional grant assistance from NABARD. According to the NABARD (Microcredit

Innovations Department), this microfinance model mobilized savings from almost 106 million households in India. It is hailed as the largest among the world's financial inclusion initiatives. This programme mainly covers women's SHGs and resulted into empowerment of rural women. NABARD also established Joint Liability Groups of small, marginal, farmers and landless labourers who were members borrowing from banks in small groups to undertake common activities and bear the liability jointly. Initially, the scheme was supported by the NABARD and the regional rural banks but was integrated with the mainstream banks from 2006 onward.

SHG Bank Linkage—The Role of Banks

As stated by Seibel (2012), the APRACA regional workshop was held in Nanjing (China) in 1986. This workshop emphasized the effectiveness of banks' linkage with self-help groups to bring about financial inclusion. The SHG-BLP was based on the lines of this programme.

Key elements advocated in the workshop were (Seibel, 2012):

- To develop the existing institutions in both formal and informal financial sectors to integrate SHGs to mainstream financial sector.
- To develop saving-based banking products to cater to the needs of the poor.
- To use NGOs to facilitate linkage of informal institutions to formal institutions.
- To developing a framework to bring about smooth co-ordination among various institutions so that the resources, infrastructure and knowhow of each institution can be utilized in a coherent manner to achieve financial inclusion.

Banks: Ultimate Financiers of Micro Credit

The non-bank finance sources of inclusion in India rely on banks for their financing in a direct or indirect way. Hence, one could perhaps find that the formal non-bank microfinance sector is just a channel of inclusive banking. Banks ultimately fund and support the institutions though the MFIs and SHGs get the credit of serving the needs of the last mile. They finance and support SHGs in various ways, i.e.,

I. Direct financing—SHGs are formed by NGOs and formal agencies but directly financed by banks. In this model, an NGO formulates the SHGs by organizing the poor. It also provides support to the SHG by way of skills training, entrepreneurial development and support to launch small productive activities. NGOs also provide training to the SHG members for book-keeping, financial transactions and lending/borrowing within the group. Banks sanction credit facility to SHGs in the name of a group on the basis of the assessment of SHGs and the recommendations of the NGOs. The latter keep a watch and ensure satisfactory functioning of the SHGs even after the linkage. This is the most popular SHG-linkage model in India where banks deal directly with individual SHGs. Other agencies can also act as SHPI.

II. This shows that the banks' contribution to microfinance is the highest in terms of live borrowers, loan portfolios and loan disbursements. As compared with the NBFC MFIs, small finance banks and NGO MFIs.

III. SHGs are formed and financed by banks. In this model, banks directly promote SHGs. With their support, the SHGs can establish small businesses to generate incomes through self-employment. Their active involvement in SHG activities by way of lending, creating financial awareness and even training the SHG officials has succeeded in removal of poverty and empowerment of the poor. Bank–SHG nexus provides a golden combination of an informal institution working in tandem with a formal mainstream partner.

IV. When banks finance NGOs, then SHGs financed by banks use NGOs as financial intermediaries. In this model, NGOs play a proactive role and act as financial intermediaries between banks and SHGs/individuals for lending. Sanction of credit involves the responsibility of repayment and bears the risk of non-payment. In this respect, it is an indirect linkage support to the SHGs. Involvement of NGOs in microcredit system has a positive influence as they are grassroot agencies with good information about borrowers. NGOs are crucial in this framework as they act as a link between the formal and informal systems. NGOs are responsible from the establishment of the SHGs up to the maturity of SHGs to take and repay credit at their own.

Challenges Faced by SHGs in India

The problems faced by the SHGs have been discussed by Seibel (2001, 2005, 2007; Dave and Seibel, 2002).

1. **Lack of standardization and governance practices:** Seibel (2012) states that NABARD has focused on quantitative growth of outreach and on credit linkages of SHGs. It has also provided funds for capacity building to promote NGOs, government organizations and banks. But group quality and operations have been left to the promoters. As a result, there is no standardized book-keeping and auditing system. internal financial intermediation of SHGs is not monitored and consolidated. Nor are the financial operations of SHGs supervised.
2. **Self-reliance**—SHGs and their members depend on banks for loans for years after their establishment. In many cases, the groups are formed only to get loans from a bank and then dissolved.
3. **Use of micro credit**—The weakest aspect of the SHG movement is that microcredit is not used for sustainable microenterprises. Members look at the SHGs as means to get petty cash for household consumption, medical and other needs. The spirit of entrepreneurship and the aspiration to come out of the vicious circle of poverty is rarely inculcated. As stated by Seibel, after the Andhra crisis (2012) there is hardly a concrete evidence of SHG members establishing successful sustainable enterprises. Over the decades, the lending by SHGs has not resulted in the SHG members promoting micro to small enterprises. The situation has not changed since then. The raison d'etre of SHG movement to encourage women to establish their own microenterprises and make them financially empowered is still a distant dream barring few exceptional cases.
4. **Scalability**—In some places, the SHG movement is been successful in consolidation of local rural women and establishing collaborative enterprises. However, these efforts are limited to a few places and stand out as exceptions. Their scalability to achieve a country-wide financial inclusion and poverty eradication is absent.
5. **Standard Practices and Data**—NABARD has taken efforts to train the SHG officials in book-keeping. However, record-keeping by SHGs is sporadic. In spite of the country-wide SHGs, presence and

ground-level operations having high value for the poverty eradication, no consolidated data on their financial transactions of SHGs have been kept. The NABARD has launched the E-Shakti drive but the data is not in public domain. Data availability is important for evaluation, improvisation and monitoring of the SHG transactions of these grassroots-level institutions.

6. **State- and district-level imbalances**—The SHGs are not free from regional imbalances in terms of their presence across the country. In the formal sector microfinance the basic criterion for financial inclusion is the bank account ownership. Ironically, the SHGs not having bank account still exist even after decades of efforts to formalize and regulate the sector.

Table 4.1 shows the state-wise percentage of SHGs having bank accounts. This percentage is not 100% at all-India level. The percentage of SHGs having bank accounts varies across the states with alarmingly low percentage in Rajasthan, Bihar and Jharkhand where the need for microlending is more due to low economic development and industrialization.

Current Issues and Challenges—MFI Sector

Competition Among the MFIs and Over-Lending

The number of NBFC–MFIs has increased exponentially with many NGOs wanting to take advantage of charging high lending rates and profits in established markets. The NGOs converted into NBFCs to get a better access to commercial funds. Because investors perceived that NBFCs had better governance structure, greater management oversight and more systemic planning, commercial lenders are more willing to provide finance to NBFCs than to NGOs (Fernando, 2004; Ghose et al., 2018; Kumar, 2012). As stated by Navin and Sinha (2019), the Andhra crisis was an eye-opener for the regulators who realized that the operations of the MFIs have to be strictly monitored to safeguard the interests of the poor. The industry concentration in the MFI sector should be controlled and smaller MFIs should be supported to prevent the prominence and misconduct by a few large institutions.

The growth and success of MFIs increased the competition and created problems for both the MFIs and their clients. The NBFC MFIs increased

Table 4.1 State-wise percentage of SHGs having bank accounts, 2019

State names	*Percentage of total SHGs having Bank A/c*
Andhra Pradesh	79.37
Assam	91.258
Bihar	40.6701
Chhattisgarh	79.3872
Gujarat	98.2902
Jharkhand	59.8706
Karnataka	95.5551
Kerala	79.2888
Madhya Pradesh	69.1469
Maharashtra	80.6729
Odisha	94.9827
Rajasthan	20.477
Tamil Nadu	98.1956
Telangana	96.1531
Uttar Pradesh	67.757
West Bengal	86.9297
Haryana	81.8079
Himachal Pradesh	85.5224
Jammu And Kashmir	99.3824
Punjab	79.9242
Uttarakhand	76.2313
Arunachal Pradesh	85.3087
Manipur	87.9409
Meghalaya	81.2637
Mizoram	88.721
Nagaland	91.6378
Sikkim	97.5343
Tripura	88.5535
Andaman And Nicobar	87.1258
Dadra And Nagar Haveli	100
Daman And Diu	56.3158
Goa	96.7968
Lakshadweep	92.8572
Puducherry	100
Grand total	79.5015

Source Derived from NRLM database https://nrlm.gov.in/

lending but they became more professional and commercial in their approach, invested less in relationship building with clients, and less focused on careful client selection, training and staff orientation. Thus, the signature MFIs developed by the pioneers of the microfinance revolution in India started waning in the post-Andhra crisis scenario of the MFI sector.

2) **Disappearing Not-for-Profit segment**

Not-for-profit MFIs are decreasing in number indicating increased commercialization in microfinance industry. Initially, the microfinance institutions used to be the 'not for profit' NGOs. MFI sector in India was characterized by these NGO MFIs that reached remote rural areas. After the restructuring following the Andhra crisis, the category of NBFC MFIs was created which are regulated by the RBI while the NGO MFIs that are not for profit are not regulated. Thus, banks and investors are reluctant to provide funds to the NGO MFIs. NGO MFIs cannot compete with the NBFC MFIs because basically the NBFCs are for profit and NGO MFIs are not. Since setting up an NBFC–MFI requires financing, many socially-minded entrepreneurs are unable to enter the sector, thereby strengthening existing monopolies (Saibal, 2019). There is a need to bring all institutions in financial inclusion landscape under a uniform regulator to prevent adverse effects of competition and unbalanced growth of the sector. Mohanty Committee recommended that corporates should be encouraged to nurture SHGs as a part of Corporate Social Responsibility (CSR) initiative.

3) **Imbalances in Geographical spread**

The Indian Microfinance Industry witnessed one of the fastest growths in the recent times. But microfinance institutions have grown in a lop-sided manner. Due to the lack of any systematic regulatory guidelines, the MFIs have preferred regions with better infrastructure and financially viable population segment. This defeats the purpose of microfinance movement. Remote regions which need microfinance due to lack of mainstream finance facilities remain neglected by the industry. The growth of microfinance institutions is often influenced by the political economy and borrowers face adverse elements of non-transparent dealings, unregulated transactions and interference by the local leaders (Saibal, *Business Today*, November 4, 2019).

Unfortunately, even after the Andhra Pradesh crisis and regulation by NABARD and RBI, the situation is relatively unchanged.

4) **Use of loans: A questionable proposition**

Use of microcredit has been a subject of debate. Many empirical studies at local level report empowerment of MFI and SHG members. However, Seibel (2012) states that borrowings from MFIs are often for purposes other than business. Loans are given for purposes like weddings, illness, etc.

Banerjee and Duflo (2011) observe that the self-employed poor usually have no specialized skills and often engaged in multiple occupations. Most businesses have a very small and inefficient scale of operation and have negligible assets. Without entry barriers, special skills and physical capital, petty businesses are not expected to grow to uplifted the poor out of poverty.

Crisis Situation Caused by the Pandemic

Liquidity Crunch

After the COVID-19 pandemic and lockdown, the MFI sector's loan portfolios have taken a turn for the worse as almost all their borrowers have suffered income loss. The Government declared a relief package targeted long term repo operations (TLTRO) of Rs. 50,000/- Crs. Most of this relief, however, is directed at larger for-profit NBFC–MFIs. Smaller organizations, societies, trusts, etc., would not benefit from it.

Organizations in the sector facing liquidity crunch and difficulties in meeting working capital requirements reportedly to be approx. Rs. 140 crores. The relief package announced by the government covers only large MFIs with investment grade rating. Thus, small and medium MFIs (which constitute approx. 80% of the MFI industry) would be excluded from it (Panda & Roy, June 17, 2020, *Business Standard*).

Crisis in the microfinance sector raises questions about its sustainability without the support of the banks and government.

Factors Leading to Vulnerability of the Sector

A financially sustainable microfinance sector implies fulfilment of minimum criterion like profitability or operational efficiency (cost-recovery). Financial efficiency requires an effective service delivery methodology and reasonable institutional and human resource competencies.

Many microfinance institutions struggle for survival because of unskilled manpower and deficient financial resources. One tends to ask whether the banks can fill these resource gaps with their financial infrastructure and competent human resources, and how a business model can be developed so that the goal of financial inclusion can be achieved? This is more so as the banks finance microlenders in one way or the other as discussed below.

Banks the Ultimate Saviours?

In India the microfinance sector is a complex conglomerate of institutions. MSMEs and poor entrepreneurs are groping for cash and liquidity for day to day expenses, while MFIs and SHGs are cash starved and wondering about their future. In this scenario stakeholders look forward to the banks to save them. The recent pandemic has shaken the edifice of microlending institutions. The banking sector is the foundation on which it stands. The inter-connectedness between MFIs and banks, and between SHGs, JLGs and banks, has come under pressure. Even the government has implemented most of the schemes like cash transfer, moratorium, lower interest rates, etc., through the banks. According to MFIN report, in 2019–2020, loans given by the banking and other financial institutions to NBFC MFIs grew by 33% over the last year.

The lockdown during the pandemic has adversely affected liquid funds of NBFC MFIs. True, the lockdown has affected entire economy, but shock to the MFI sector is worse than the banks because the MFI borrowers primarily from the worst affected informal sectors. Also, the average duration of MFI loans is shorter than the bank loans and the repayment is mostly in cash. Banks provide finance to the MFIs at a rate much lower than the lending rate charged by the MFIs for their borrowers. This is really like an acid wash for those who thought that banks have become redundant in the new situation with the emergence of various intermediaries in the regular as well as microfinance sectors.

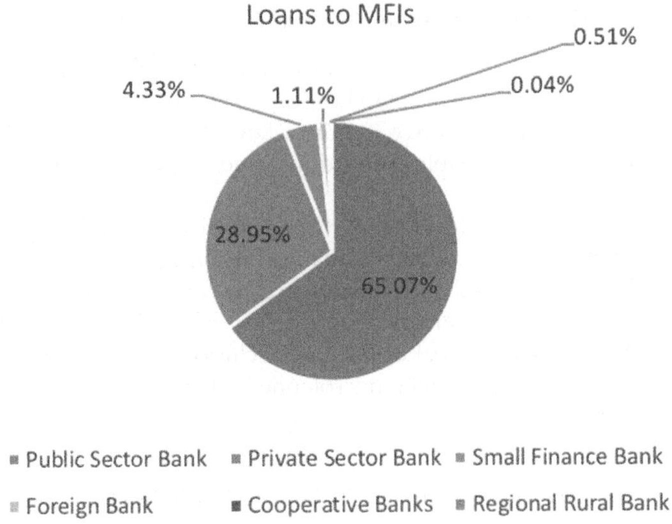

Fig. 4.7 Loans to MFIs by banks (*Source* Based on *Annual Reports, 2009–10 to 2018–19 NABARD,* www.nabard.org)

The crisis has emphasized the role of commercial state-owned banks for the sustainability and resilience of the economy and welfare of the poor.

In India, two SBLP models have emerged over time. In the first model, the bank acts as an SHG promoting an institution (SHPI). In the second model, some intermediary NGO acts as an SHG promoting institution between the bank and the SHG. Alternatively, the bank finances MFI on a large scale and complies by its priority sector lending norm. The intricate structure of linkages among financial institutions can be captured by using a network representation of financial systems (Fig. 4.7).

In India, the microfinance sector is undergoing many upheavals, e.g. Andhra Pradesh Crisis, regulatory reforms, bank licensing of MFIs, pandemic shock, etc. Thus, the Indian microfinance sector has a bearing on the financial inclusion (Purkayastha et al., 2014).

How Resilient Are Financial Networks to Stress?

According to the RBI database (2020), bank lending outstanding to the aggregate NBFC sector is Rs. 7 lakh crore. The 54 NBFC–MFIs, that are members of MFIN, have drawn around Rs. 35,000 crore from banks and about Rs. 19,000 crore is from other development institutions and NBFCs.

The dependence of the non-bank microfinance sector on the banks raises important questions. The NBFC microfinance is for profit and not cheaper than mainstream and vulnerable to shocks. It leads one to explore alternatives in the so called mainstream bank finance.

Many studies confirm that reliance on microfinance for poverty alleviation is risky. In most countries, the microfinance sector remains negligible as compared with the need for finance for uplifting the poor. Many developing countries in Africa have achieved financial depth by expansion of inclusive banking services which is important to reduce poverty. One should accept that the microfinance sector is not the holy grail of financial inclusion.

The banking sector with its social banking outreach and advanced technology can develop a business model inclusive of the poor. Non-bank microfinance institutions play a supportive role of special purpose vehicles or channels to implement inclusive banking.

Annexure: Credit Bureaus—Working and Effectiveness for Inclusion

Credit bureaus are specialized institutions to prepare consumer credit reports and maintain the database needed for decision-making by the microlenders. Credit Bureau can create a complete database and profile of potential borrowers. They can collect the data from multiple credit disbursing institutions, banking and non-banking institutions.[1] Commercial banks can have access to the data collected by the credit bureaus. New technology can be used to access the credit history and data from Aadhaar-linked accounts, MFIs, NGOs and SHGs. In India, four credit bureaus work for the microfinance sector, i.e. Equifax India, High Mark Credit Information Services Pvt. Ltd., Experian and CIBIL.™

Equifax provides a customer credit report with the potential customer's identification and contact details, credit summary, credit utilization and latest activity in relation to credit. Account details that mention credit

[1] https://tribune.com.pk/story/2109595/2-credit-bureau-aims-enhance-financial-inclusion/.

accounts from the past and present, along with data connected to the repayment track for each of the possessed accounts are also included. Similarly, CIBIL offers market insights, company credit information reports, bureau analyser, portfolio reviews and TransUnion Score to benefit and guide various MFI institutions.

Highmark MFI bureau provides a number of products along with services such as portfolio management, PERFORM score, geo-analytics consulting, alerts, etc.

Experian offers different products that supply to microfinance bodies customer targeting, collections, customer management, business information services and analytical solutions.

Usefulness for Lenders

Although the credit bureau is a new development in India, it will be of great help to reduce the risk of default of the thin filed microcredit borrower.

In sub-Saharan Africa,[2] credit bureaus have helped to enhance microlending by providing accurate information on client credibility. They help the lenders handle the information asymmetry and thus help borrowers as the lenders are willing to provide loans at a justifiable interest rate.

Credit bureaus can also help prevent over-borrowing by the borrowers and improve availability and accessibility of credit. A recent study of 129 countries established that creditor protection rights and availability of information-sharing institutions promoted inclusive financial growth.[3] Private and public credit bureaus promoted private credit development in developing countries more than in developed countries. They provide information and services that lenders use to assess the affordability and creditworthiness of prospective customers, as well as verify applicants. An increase in credit reference bureau services is expected to improve access to relevant customer information, thereby increasing access to credit, especially in developing countries where credit transaction information

[2] https://www.ifc.org/wps/wcm/connect/REGION__EXT_Content/Regions/Sub-Saharan+Africa/Advisory+Services/AccessFinance/Credit+Bureaus+Program/.

[3] https://compuscan.co.za/2020/02/17/how-a-credit-bureau-affects-financial-inclusion/.

is difficult to obtain. Credit bureaus in South Africa are required by law to give the citizens one free credit report every year.

In India, the credit bureaus for microfinance are a new development and the utilization is limited due to the paucity of data of the borrowers and their credit history. New developments in data analytics and Aadhaar/UID requirements hold a promise of greater data availability and use of these credit bureaus and their ratings. In the future if credit bureaus successfully work for the sector, then it will facilitate microlending by banks as they will be able to discard the issue of collecting credit history and loan monitoring of the microcredit segment.

References

Dave, H., & Seibel, H. (2002). *Commercial aspects of self-help group banking in India: A study of bank transaction costs*. Working Paper, No. 2002, 7. Koln, Germany: University of Cologne, Development Research Center. Available at: https://core.ac.uk/reader/6591894.

Duflo, E., & Banerjee, A. (2011). *Poor economics* (Vol. 619). Public Affairs.

Fernando, N. A. (2004). *Micro success story?: Transformation of nongovernment organizations into regulated financial institutions*. Asian Development Bank.

Ghose, B., Paliar, S. J., & Mena, L. (2018). Does legal status affect performance of microfinance institutions?: Empirical evidence from india. *Vision, 22*(3), 316–328.

Joshi, et al. (2012). *Report on management practises of microfinance institutions in India*. Study sponsored by World Economic Forum.

Kumar, M. (2012). *Crisis at the bottom of the pyramid: A case study of micro-FINANCE in India*. Available at SSRN 2177290.

MFIN Report Q4. (January and March 2020). *Microfinance Institutions Network*. Retrieved from https://mfinindia.org/assets/upload_image/news/pdf/Press%20Release%20-%20Q4%202019-20%20Micrometer.pdf.

NABARD, Microcredit Innovations Department (https://www.nabard.org/about-departments.aspx?id=5&cid=477).

NABARD, Various Annual Reports, 2009–10 to 2018–19. Retrieved from www.nabard.org.

Navin, N., & Sinha, P. (2019). Market structure and competition in the Indian microfinance sector. *Vikalpa, 44*(4), 167–181.

NRLM database-on https://nrlm.gov.in/.

Panda, S., & Roy, A. (2020). Coronavirus impact: RBI's TLTRO 2.0 gets cold-shoulder from banks. *Business Standard*. Dated April 24, 2020. https://www.business-standard.com/article/finance/coronavirus-impact-rbi-s-tltro-2-0-gets-cold-shoulder-from-banks-120042301666_1.html.

Purkayastha, D., Tripathy, T., & Das, B. (2014). The impact of regulations on microfinance industry: A strategic perspective. *IUP Journal of Business Strategy, 11*(3).

RBI. (2011). *Report of the Sub-Committee of the Central Board of Directors of Reserve Bank of India to Study Issues and Concerns in the MFI Sector*. Malegam, S.Y.H. Reserve Bank of India. New Delhi.

Saibal, P. (2019, November 4). Four major risks facing microfinance in India. *Business Today*. https://www.businesstoday.in/opinion/columns/microfinance-in-india-four-major-risks-facing-the-sector-rbi-nbfc-sector-banking-sector/story/388372.html.

Seibel, H. D. (2001). *SHG banking: A financial technology for reaching marginal areas and the very poor*. University of Cologne.

Seibel, H. D. (2005). *SHG banking in India: The evolution of a rural financial innovation* (Working Paper No. 2005, 9).

Seibel, H. D. (2007). *From informal microfinance to linkage banking: Putting theory into practice, and practice into theory* (Working Paper No. 2007, 1a).

Seibel, H. D. (2012). An approach towards self-reliance and sustainability of the SHG sector: SHG sector own control. *The microFINANCE*, 1.

SIDBI, EQUIFAX, Microfinance Pulse. (June 2019, January 2020).*Reports*. http://14.143.90.243/sidbi/en/microfinance-pulse.

CHAPTER 5

Inclusive Banking: A Political Economy Approach

For any country, the success of inclusive institutions depends on the broader economic and political environment. In India, the prevailing policy initiatives like PMJDY and PMMY have helped in opening the accounts and spreading the access to banks. Now to take financial inclusion to a next level, the policy should focus on increasing the usage of accounts and ensuring the sustainability of inclusive finance. This requires identifying the existing gaps and preparing for the new challenges. The first step is to deal with the questions arising out of the present inclusive finance scenario. Some of the pertinent questions are: First, is there a need for numerous institutions in financial inclusion space? Second, despite a large number of institutions already active in financial inclusion, why do some areas lack inclusion or under usage bank accounts? Third, in spite of a number of institutions, why do the informal sector moneylenders thrive? This chapter explores the political economy approach to answer these questions.

Political Economy of Financial Inclusion—The Context

Political economy approach analyses how members of a society interact with one another, compete for power and make decisions to ensure their survival and position (Whitfield & Therkildsen, 2011).

L. Kulkarni and V. C. Joshi, *Inclusive Banking In India*,
https://doi.org/10.1007/978-981-33-6797-5_5

In the context of financial inclusion, it considers the dynamic relationships among various institutions in financial inclusion universe. It is useful because it helps to formulate more effective intervention by policy-makers through a focus on 'what works' rather than normative ideals of governance (Duncan & Williams, 2012).

Global literature talks about two political economy approaches to financial inclusion. One is the market-led approach where the government tries to reform the system with the help of donor agencies. After the global financial crisis in 2008, instead of relying on special microfinance institutions, the governments have been emphasizing restructuring the financial systems to make them more inclusive of the poor sections of the population (World Bank, 2008). This policy requires public sector banks to cater to the needs of the agricultural and rural areas neglected by the private financial institutions. In India, this policy has been adopted by the government through priority sector lending norms, interest rate regulations and subsidization of credit. This approach sees the government as an enabler of market infrastructure necessary for inclusive finance.[1] This approach of achieving financial inclusion through directing public sector banks to lend to the sectors specified as priority sectors by the government is called an interventionist or activist approach.[2]

As against this, the Market Development approach acknowledges the role of governments in building economic environment conducive to financial inclusion. Agencies like Department for International Development, DFID (Unsworth & Williams, 2011; Yanguas & Hulme, 2014) and World Bank (Fritz et al., 2009) have been relying on political economy approach of interplay of interest groups and incentives to formulate strategies for effective policy interventions in country-specific context.

Getting away from a regularized environment towards neo-liberalism, banks sometimes find it difficult to sustain the market pressures. On the one hand, governments adopted market liberalization and reforms in financial sector in recent years termed as the modernist approach. On the other hand, an alternative set of specialized microfinance institutions

[1] The role of Government in inclusive finance is discussed in the next chapter.

[2] Facing up to the political realities of financial inclusion Time for donors to re-think their approach? Oxford Policy Management October 2013.

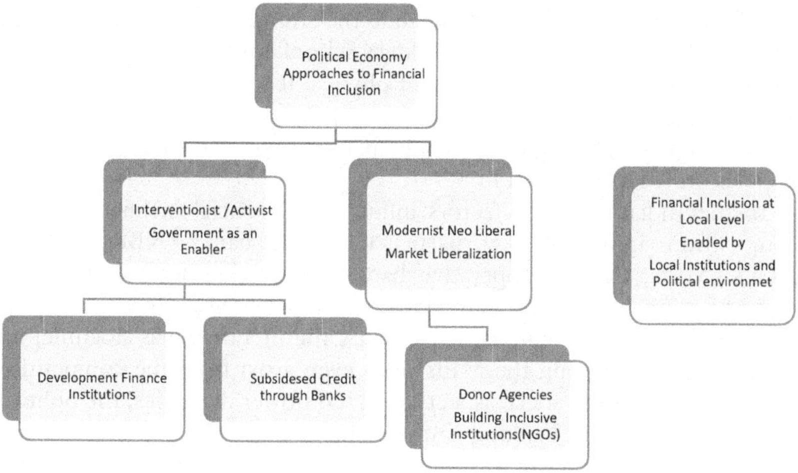

Fig. 5.1 Political Economy Approaches to Financial Inclusion (*Source* Compiled by the authors)

encouraged by the donor agencies through financing NGOs led to the growth of microfinance sector.

To achieve effective financial inclusion, international donor agencies have to associate with the governments of recipient countries. The policy of financial inclusion should not be constrained by conflicting modernist or activist ideologies. It should transcend them and recognize the need to adopt and adapt to the heterogeneous socio-eco-political institutional environment at local level. In the Indian context, this approach is relevant as the success of financial inclusion depends on the local socio-political factors. Figure 5.1 summarizes the different approaches.

Political Economy: Factors Determining Access to Finance

The political economy factors influencing the access to financial inclusion depend on quality of political institutions in each country. According to Martinez (2011), a complex combination and interaction of political competition, vote banks, terms of the governments, local power politics, federal political relations, etc., are at work.

Other non-economic factors include the strength of legal rights index, level of cell phone usage and secondary school enrolment.

Cell phone use and availability of physical technological infrastructure are regarded as the most important factors to overcome geographical condition and cost to provide financial services to the unbanked population (Martinez, 2011).

In the Indian context, factors influencing financial inclusion are the competition among market participants (like banks, NBFCs- MFIs, NGO -MFIs, RRBs, cooperative banks, etc.,), their power dynamics, regional composition and non-economic factors (like voter bank politics, caste/religion dimension). In India, the literature has documented the competition among the MFIs. However, apart from the competition among the MFIs and social aspects of SHGs power dynamics, the political economy of inclusive banking is not examined.

The current chapter delves into the effects of the competition among various institutions, the political economy behind regional disparity in financial inclusion and the rationale for informal sources of lending.

Political Economy Approach in the Context of Financial Inclusion in India

Interaction and Interdependence Among Inclusive Finance Providers

The inclusive finance sector in India consists of many players at different layers as seen already. In 2019, it included over 200 MFIs, over 66 lakh SHGs, 43 RRBs, 6 Payments Banks, in addition to small finance banks, agricultural co-operative banks and government schemes implemented through commercial banks. Even though at the country level the number is large, the local level scene is different. At the level of a village or ward in the urban area, the inclusive institutions are few and have their own identity with the local customers. Thus, the market turns into an oligopoly where each player has a market segment to cater to and the strategies, products, services and frills offered to depend on the other players' strategies.

Each department has various schemes under which the specified beneficiaries get subsidized credit, finance, etc., like the Handloom Sector Technology Upgradation Fund (TUF). These schemes are implemented via scheduled commercial banks, cooperative banks and regional rural banks. But the schemes often overlap. The local power politics determines the effectiveness, group of beneficiaries and actual benefit percolated to the beneficiary. Within the government, various departments do not want the schemes under them to be universalized.

As put forward by Zingales and Rajan (2003), interest groups influence the financial sector development and also whether and how the reforms will be adopted in practice.

Government Initiatives and the Donor Agencies

Local political constituencies or voters demand the governance reform in the system by the government; for example, in India, people want subsidized loans. These reforms are implemented through the state-owned banks and financial institutions like NABARD, and hence, the donors should support them. However, donors find it difficult to monitor these key stakeholders in the market reform. At the government level, the donors may make conditional grants specifying rates and other terms and may make them obligatory. On the other hand, it could be left to an individual organization to decide the terms. Hence, the donors prefer to operate within an existing 'feasible reform space' by funding activist institutions (Johnson & Williams, 2016).

The activist institutions (MFIs, NGOs, SHG Federations, etc.,) get grants from the donors as the initiatives are more concrete and able to be monitored as compared with the government schemes. Until now the funding to the activist institutions was through social investors and donors. New developments promise shifting the emphasis on funding from social investors through equity and bond markets. In the latest budget, the Finance Minister has announced the establishment of a social stock exchange in India. These developments are discussed in Chapter 7.

Competition Among the Agents

Another aspect of political economy is the competition among the microfinance institutions and the changing structure of the industry. The latter has undergone changes in the ownership, regulation and mission of MFIs. These changes are well documented with various measures of competition being applied to them (Armendáriz & Szafarz, 2011; Assefa et al., 2013; Nair, 2010; Navin & Sinha, 2019).

Competition also exists between the formal and informal sources of microlending and also among the various formal institutions providing microlending.

Mookherjee and Motta (2016) study competition between informal sector moneylenders and MFIs. Concerned about the portfolio risk, the MFIs' repayment requirements are rigid and the borrowers have to seek informal credit from moneylenders to repay the loans. This defeats both the social and the financial objectives of MFIs as with increasing reliance on informal sector loans the borrowers become more and more vulnerable and the risk to MFIs increases. In the financial inclusion space in India, there are banks and MFIs. Hence, the questions are: What are the effects of competition on the stakeholders, i.e. banks, MFIs and the borrowers? Does the availability of MFI loans affect the overall microlending by the banks? Do the banks and MFIs overlap in providing microfinance?

Symbiotic Relation Between Banks and MFIs

In India, the MFIs and banks are inter-dependent and hence instead of competition a symbiotic relationship prevails. The extant literature considers its four aspects, viz. (i) crowding-in, (ii) multiple borrowing by clients, (iii) potential synergies between banks and MFIs, and (iv) how competition changes MFI portfolio structure.

Does crowding-in exist? Competition between the moneylenders and MFIs exists and results in crowding-in defeating the purpose of microfinance. On the other hand, the entry of banks in microlending arena has a positive effect as it results in MFIs diverting toward poorer borrowers and small-sized loans, thus potentially weeding away the moneylenders. Cull et al. (2009, 2011) observe that bank entry pushes MFIs to focus on smaller loans to poorer clientele. They also find that MFIs show greater outreach when faced with higher and more concentrated bank competition.

Multiple borrowing by clients: As there appeared many cases of borrowing from multiple MFIs, across sub-Saharan Africa, Bolivia, India, etc., MFIs refused to cater to a client with an outstanding loan elsewhere. However, determining whether clients had outstanding loans is both costly and difficult, as there is little information sharing across the entire financial services industry (Armendariz & Morduch, 2010). The same issue arises in the case of bank–MFI loans. With the banks in India now lending under various government schemes, the issue of borrowing from multiple lenders is common.

Potential bank-MFI synergies: If the borrowers of the banks and MFIs overlap, then the borrowers can use MFI loans to finance bank loans creating greater demand for both types of lending. However, widespread incidence of this practice has the danger of systemic risk in case of shocks to the economy similar to COVID-19 pandemic where the entire segment of financial institutions linked by risky portfolios could collapse.

Changes in MFI portfolios: When banks enter microlending business, the MFIs feel the competition and divert their portfolios from richer non-poor borrowers to poorer borrowers needing small/microloans (Cull et al., 2009, 2011).

Implications of the relation between banks and MFIs depend on the extent of development of a country.

In India, banks operate through MFIs to curtail the operating costs of meeting the microlending targets. They support microlending by MFIs and SHGs through loan guarantees and refinancing but are hardly recognized for their contribution to financial inclusion. When MFIs and SHGs deliver the funds, they capture the limelight for being benevolent messiahs for helping the poor while the banks bear the ultimate financial burden. On the other hand, financing MFIs helps the banks meet their priority sector lending targets. It is customary for them to include the MFI customers in the bank balance sheets under the priority sector lending. Thus, in India, MFIs and banks exist in symbiotic relation rather than competing with each other.

Competition Within the MFI Sector—Impact on MFIs

MFIs compete amongst themselves for clients as well as donors and funds. So they face challenges of retaining customers and remaining financially feasible or profitable to attract donors. Like competitive oligopolistic firms, MFIs have to study the competitors' behaviour and client preferences to adopt a business strategy. Only those institutions which prudently provide services and products demanded by the clients (e.g. day care for members' children, preschool and medical care facilities, etc.) can survive. In some countries, competition among the institutions and pressure to remain profitable results in targeting the bankable clients. Studies have documented the competition between the banks and MFIs. In countries like Madagascar, if the MFIs know that the banks are located near the potential or existing MFI borrowers, then they charge lower interest rates and make the terms of borrowing easier for the borrowers (Baraton & Leon, 2018). This factor may become outdated with the spread of electronic and mobile banking and finance.

Competition Within the MFI Sector—Adverse Effect on Clients

Over-indebtedness: Competition defeats the very purpose of MFIs and SHGs which is to support the underprivileged and to help them achieve their aspirations. An overly competitive financial inclusion market leads to over-indebtedness of the clients due to easy availability of microloans offered by the institutions vying for a market share. Competition amongst MFIs as well as with SHGs has emerged in India. Empirical studies report that MFIs have common set of clients, members attending multiple MFI meetings in a day and members borrowing from one MFI to repay the loans of another MFI. The ground level loan officers generally know about these multiple borrowings. The studies in developing countries like Bolivia, Uganda, Bangladesh, etc., also have reported similar competition among the MFIs (Rhyne, 2002). The development of credit bureaus has in some measure curtailed these practices.

Discerning customers gain access to a greater choice and so they become more demanding and discerning. In India, we see the fast tracking of the individual lending approach with the entry of Non-Banking Finance Companies in the microfinance market segment.

Competition among the MFIs: Concentration and Exploitation: A competitive market is generally regarded as a virtue rendering market clearing price, normal profits and minimum dead weight loss. However, competition in a special case of incomplete markets with information asymmetry and inadequate institutions may not be virtuous. Empirical evidence exhibits reduction in client welfare due to excess competition among the MFIs.

When the market is competitive, there are no barriers to entry. It replicates an elastic demand curve and credit can be provided to all those who are willing to borrow. In this case, the price or interest rate cannot be increased by the provider MFI as it will push the demand for its loans to zero as the borrowers will shift to another MFI (Fig. 5.2). This is an ideal

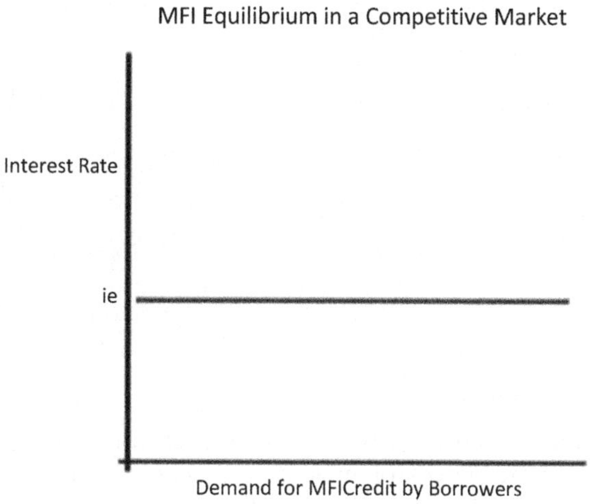

Fig. 5.2 Demand for Microfinance in a Competitive Market (*Source* Compiled by the authors)

situation.

The market for microlending is characterized by information asymmetry. The lender does not know the credit history of the borrower because of incomplete markets with inadequate institutional set-up. Additionally, borrowers can go for multiple borrowings with no intention to pay back. This improves the welfare of some borrowers but only for a short period. It works ultimately against inclusive finance as the MFIs, presuming this default, start charging higher interest rates and the welfare of the poor and honest clients is hampered leading them to informal moneylenders.

This problem arising due to information asymmetry termed as 'lemons problem' is discussed by Hoff and Stieglitz (1997), Kranton and Swamy (1999), Van Tassel (2014), Guha and Roy Chowdhury (2013), etc.

New Dimensions of Competition Among Microlenders in India

In India, the competition among the financial inclusion providers has a unique dimension.

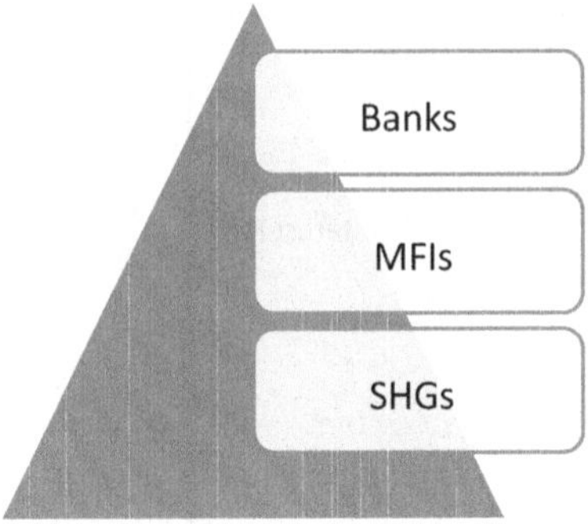

Fig. 5.3 Structure of Microlending Sector in India (*Source* Compiled by the authors)

Banks refinance and fund the non-bank institutions for microlending and also act as facilitators of government schemes. So, as depicted in Fig. 5.3, each layer is co-dependent on the other, i.e. banks are dependent on MFIs and SHGs to implement the microlending schemes to achieve their targets. The MFIs and NGOs engage as organizations/federations of SHGs providing them support.

Banks implement their microfinance goals through MFIs, NGOs and SHGs. This network facilitates lending and monitoring microloans. MFIs and NGOs are dependent on the banks for refinancing and capital. Thus, in the Indian microlending sector, the competition is among the institutions existing at each layer of this pyramid and not much across the institutions prevailing at different layers of the pyramid. Hence, co-dependency prevails over competition. Literature on the microfinance industry focuses on the competition between banks and MFIs but it is not applicable to Indian scenario.

Method of Interest Calculation Leading to High Effective Rate

Methods of charging and application of interest do make a difference in the actual rate charged. The interest rates are below the RBI's permissible rates. According to the MFIN Âµm Report (March 2020), the rates are around 24–25%, while the cost of capital is around 14–15%.

MFIs cannot diversify beyond the microfinance market. Thus, to survive in a competitive environment, they cannot search new segments but have to adopt strategies like price differentiation. The literature reports downward pressure on MFI lending rates due to competition (Meyer, 2002; Rhyne, 2002).

In India, the price of microlending is a controversial issue. The NABARD and RBI have already capped the maximum interest rate to be charged on microlending. Nevertheless, some practices are followed by the MFIs resulting in higher effective rates. The studies do not report a price reduction due to competition among the microlending institutions. As per MFIN report, the MFIs abide by the interest rate cap as per the RBI regulation and the lending rates by most of them are within the range of 19.8–27.2% (MFIN, 2016). Reports find an inverse relation between the size of MFIs in terms of gross loan portfolio and the lending rate signifying economies of scale (MFIN, 2016). It implies that large MFIs earn normal profits and transfer the efficiency gains to the borrowers. Lending rates of small MFIs remain higher than large MFIs due to lower scale of operations (Hartarska et al., 2013).

Price-Based Differentiation Is Neither Desirable Nor Needed

For decades together, the regulatory norms required the banks to charge different interest rates for different segments of borrowers. Low interest rate for the poor borrower was expected to be cross-subsidized. Currently, though differential interest rates are done away with and there are no interest rate ceilings, government schemes clearly mention lower rates for microlending. MFIs charge lending rates that ensure a viable business model for them and borrowers demand loans at this rate. The repayment of MFIs loan has never been a problem. In this background, the argument that banks have to provide finance to the poor at lower interest rates is not justified.

MFIs charge higher interest rates than the priority sector lending rates charged by banks. Because of the subsidized interest rates for microlending, banks are not motivated to increase the outreach and the borrower ends up with the MFI (or worse with the moneylender), ultimately paying a higher rate. This system can change only over a time as the institutional framework depends on socio-political interest groups that are difficult to change within a short period with policy interventions. An interesting example quoted in FICCI/M-CRIL Report (2011) is that of the subsidized agricultural credit in India. The subsidized rural credit and loan waivers are regarded as 'rights' and have become the rule of the day. An indirect fallout of this perspective is that the banks consider agricultural lending as a mandatory burden as they expect that the formal regulatory structure will not be followed and they will end up with much larger obligations (Johnson, 2013).

If we compare the rates of rural credit institutions like district credit cooperative banks, etc., we find that although they charge an interest rate based on financial feasibility, the rates are around 10–12% (M-CRIL, 2011). So if the banks are not expected to charge artificially low rates on these loans, it will motivate them to perceive this portfolio as one of the financially viable portfolios. The working of this model is provided in Chapter 8.

New dimensions: Earlier many studies reported that distance from bank branch or MFIs office as one of the factors affecting competition (Rajan & Zingales, 2003). It will become increasingly redundant due to the spread of mobile banking and e-banking. With the availability of internet facilities across the nook and corner of India, physical proximity to a bank or MFI is not an important factor in competition.

Affinity to social community: In India and other developing countries of Asia and Africa, the sense of belonging and affinity with the community is strong. Even if a bank or MFI loan is available, people may prefer to borrow from the moneylender because he belongs to their community. The power of self-affinity groups should be utilized by the banks to reach these communities. In India, many a time the issue is not of the availability of banking or access to banking, but of the banks getting access into the communities and acceptance by the people.

Political Economy: Reasons of Regional Disparity in Microlending

The current problems of inclusive finance in India are underutilization of accounts and regional disparity in institutions. As shown above, activities of MFIs are distributed unevenly across the states. The activity of top ten MFIs in terms of loan outstanding and average loan outstanding per account is concentrated in Tamil Nadu, West Bengal, Bihar, UP, Odisha and Karnataka (Fig. 5.4). In the remaining states, they are much below the average. Why does this disparity exist even after decades of policy effort?

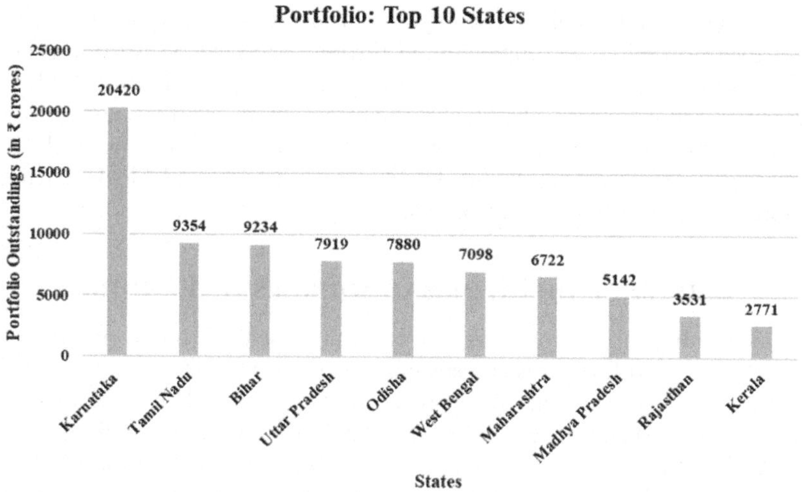

Fig. 5.4 State-wise Portfolio of Microfinance Institutions in Top 10 States (*Source* Derived from *Bharat Microfinance Report, 2019*, p. 22)

The reasons can be found in the political economy in Indian context.

For instance, one tenet of political economy of financial inclusion is that the financial system is influenced by the limited number of powerful groups of people for their own benefit and this domination should be regulated (Bates, 2014). This phenomenon is evident in India in the case of RRBs, cooperatives and MFIs. Another tenet of political economy states that the rent seeking by dominant groups leads to influencing the policy which results in reinforcement of the biased social and economic order. In India, the MFIs and SHGs are more active in areas where local political parties support them. In regions where the local population is scattered and the vote bank can be tied together and nurtured based on some issues other than inclusion, the population is in abject poverty and the inclusive activities are neglected. In El Salvador, Honduras and Guatemala, Cabello (2007) argues that due to governmental ignorance the regions remained underdeveloped and the cross border emigration resulted in overseas remittances. This dis-incentivized the governments to actively implement development policies for them. The regional divide is not superficial just reflecting convenience due to geographical factors or proximity. Power politics is often at play.

In some countries like those of sub-Saharan Africa, the quick-fix financial inclusion initiatives implemented through specialized institutions are used as means to seek voters' support (Girma & Shortland, 2008). Wherever the population is unorganized and fragmented or no interest groups or activism exists, there is a dearth of inclusive institutions. This results in politically and economically advanced states, districts and blocks having more financial inclusion than others.

Existence of Informal Sources of Lending

Moneylending profession is as old as money itself. In India, one of the puzzles of microfinance is the sustenance of moneylenders and informal sources of finance in spite of outreach by banks and MFIs. The reasons for this phenomenon are stated in the book by Aloysius Fernandez of MyRADA, a pioneering microfinance NGO in South India (2018). According to him, group and community affinities are important factors influencing people's decisions. Eradication of moneylenders and depiction of a stereo-typical exploitative moneylender are the perception of the outsiders who are often oblivious to the equations of the local community politics. People still prefer moneylenders over banks and other formal MFIs because this formality is not a virtue for them. Some factors influencing small borrowers are as follows:

1. Small ticket size: The amount of money required by people can be very small, i.e. a few hundred rupees. This small loan can be availed of only from informal sources like friends, relatives or moneylenders. Due to the ad hoc nature of their employment or seasonal employment, the need for small but frequent and urgent sums is always felt by rural as well as urban poor. These sums are used for petty consumption purposes and cannot be borrowed from MFIs or even SHGs, let alone from the banks. The data on MFIs shows that their average loan size in India is approximately Rs. 20000/-. The moneylenders can lend much smaller amounts informally. The moneylenders also disburse the loans immediately without procedural hassles.
2. Flexible collaterals: The demand for liquid cash to seek subsistence is the key force making the poor beeline the moneylenders. The latter provide immediate cash for a convenient collateral and provide a

solution to the thin-filed no collateral clientele. For instance, it was revealed recently by Ravik Bhattacharya and Joyprakash Das (*The Indian Express*, April 17, 2020) that in Jharkhand and the district of Purulia in West Bengal families have handed over their ration cards as collateral to moneylenders for amounts they borrowed years ago. This was revealed when the officials approached them to announce the state government schemes of free ration under public distribution system for six months. Villagers who needed money urgently for illness, weddings, etc., adopted in this practice for decades.

3. Flexible instalments: Instalments in the informal system are often flexible, frequency is greater and the amounts are small. This flexibility is convenient as the poor borrowers have always dearth of liquid cash. For these advantages, they are ready to pay the price of lifelong repayments, often intergenerational repayments. This is an exploitative system, but may not be perceived as burdensome, if one is bothered about only the current instalment at a time. It is the liquid cash which matters.
4. The advantage of familiarity and relationship: During the pandemic, the dependence of people on the informal sector credit has increased. There is no way one can estimate this activity accurately. The informal sector sources range from relatives to NBFCs. Allen et al. (2007) found that in India people abide by social reputation and societal ties which can be utilized effectively for a borrower's screening and credit monitoring. For example, in sub-Saharan Africa, relationship lending is strong with reputational networks built around culturally connected groups. Harnessing of local 'soft' information through long-term relationships is the most important prerequisite to achieve financial inclusion in bank-led economies (Honohan & Beck, 2007).

Studies point out that if banks neglect these networks and keep on financing large borrowers in a regular market, they may miss a lucrative market.

Inclusive Baking Depends on the Ideology of the State Regarding the Private Sector

Today, the privatization of the public sector banks is being debated in India. This would raise the issue of how the inclusive finance policies would be carried over by the privatized banks. In any country, the relation of the government with the private sector is often reflected from the banking sector reforms. The manner in which they translate themselves and penetrate up to the grass-root level shows the political economy of the state's relation with the private sector (Boone, 2005). Empirical studies show that the power dynamics between the state and private capital affect financial inclusion (Cabello, 2007). This power dynamic is complex as the inter-relations between the two are steered through the elite in the private sector. Also, the state is dependent on the private capital for tax revenue.

Since 2013-14, the government has revived inclusive banking with the JAM trinity implemented through banks. These initiatives have been implemented earlier through the banking channel. The basic question is whether banks treat this business as a mandatory requirement or see any potential for a new business model in it.

The political economy approach points out that the banking sector framework depends on the ideology of the state. Political pressures, lobbies and interest groups determine the implementation of best practices. This has been experienced by the breach of lending practices and frauds in many countries including India.

References

Allen, F., Chakrabarti, R., De, S., Qian, J., & Qian, M. (2007). The financial system capacities in China and India. SSRN1260947.

Armendáriz, B., & Morduch, J. (2010). *The economics of microfinance*. MIT press.

Armendáriz, B., & Szafarz, A. (2011). On mission drift in microfinance institutions. In *The handbook of microfinance* (pp. 341–366).

Assefa, E., Hermes, N., & Meesters, A. (2013). Competition and the performance of microfinance institutions. *Applied Financial Economics, 23*(9), 767–782.

Baraton, P., & Leon, F. (2018). *Do banks and microfinance institutions compete? Micro evidence from Madagascar*. http://wwwfr.uni.lu/recherche/fdef/crea/publications2/discussion_paper.

Bates, R. H. (2014). *Markets and states in tropical Africa: The political basis of agricultural policies*. University of California Press.

Bhattacharya, R., & Das, J. (2020). Lockdown relief reveals Purulia secret: PDS cards as loan collateral. *The Indian Express*, dated 17 April 2020. https://indianexpress.com/article/coronavirus/bengal-purulia-lockdown-pds-card-ration-covid-19–6366108/.

Boone, C. (2005). State, capital, and the politics of banking reform in sub-Saharan Africa. *Comparative Politics*, 401–420.

Cabello, R. R. (2007). *Microbiologia y parasitologia humana/Microbiology and human parasitology: Bases etiologicas de las enfermedades infecciosas y parasitarias/Etiological basis of infectious and parasitic diseases*. Ed. Médica Panamericana.

Cull, R., Demirgüç-Kunt, A., & Morduch, J. (2009). Microfinance meets the market. *Journal of Economic perspectives, 23*(1), 167–192.

Cull, R., Demirgüç-Kunt, A., & Morduch, J. (2011). Does regulatory supervision curtail microfinance profitability and outreach? *World Development, 39*(6), 949–965.

DFID (2004). *"What is pro-poor growth and why do we need to know?" Pro-poor growth briefing note 1*. Department for International Development.

Duncan, A., & Williams, G. (2012). Making development assistance more effective through using political-economy analysis: What has been done and what have we learned? *Development Policy Review, 30*(2), 133–148.

Fernandez, A. (2018). The Myrada experience, 50 years of leaning, Myrada.

Fritz, V., Kaiser, K., & Levy, B. (2009). *Problem-driven governance and political economy analysis: Good practice framework.*

Girma, S., & Shortland, A. (2008). The political economy of financial development. *Oxford Economic Papers, 60*(4), 567–596.

Guha, B., & Chowdhury, P. R. (2013). Micro-finance competition: Motivated micro-lenders, double-dipping and default. *Journal of Development Economics, 105*, 86–102.

Hartarska, V., Shen, X., & Mersland, R. (2013). Scale economies and input price elasticities in microfinance institutions. *Journal of Banking & Finance, 37*(1), 118–131.

Hoff, K., & Stiglitz, J. E. (1997). Moneylenders and bankers: Price-increasing subsidies in a monopolistically competitive market. *Journal of Development Economics, 52*(2), 429–462.

Honohan, P., & Beck, T. (2007). *Making finance work for Africa*. The World Bank.

Ianchovichina, E., & Lundstrom, S. (2008). *Inclusive growth analytics: Framework and application*. The World Bank.

Johnson, S. (2013). From microfinance to inclusive financial markets: The challenge of social regulation. *Oxford Development Studies, 41*(supl), S35–S52.

Johnson, S., & Williams, R. (2016, September). The political economy of financial inclusion: Tailoring donor policy to fit. *Development Policy Review, 34*(5), 721–743. Retrieved from: SSRN: https://ssrn.com/abstract=2817139 or http://dx.doi.org/10.1111/dpr.12170.

Kranton, R., & Swamy, A. (1999). The hazards of piecemeal reform: British civil courts and the credit market in colonial India. *Journal of Development Economics, 58,* 1–24.

Martinez, M. V. (2011). *The political economy of increased financial access* (Doctoral dissertation, Georgetown University).

Mas, I., & Kabir, K. (2008, June). "Banking on mobiles: why, how, for whom?" Consultative group to assist the poor.

M-CRIL Microfinance Review 2011: Anatomy of a Crisis (2011). https://www.findevgateway.org/paper/2011/12/m-cril-microfinance-review-2011-anatomy-crisis-executive-summary.

Mendoza, R. U., & Thelen, N. (2008). Innovations to make markets more inclusive for the poor. *Development Policy Review, 26*(4), 427–458.

Mersland, R., & Strøm, R. Ø. (2010). Microfinance mission drift? *World Development, 38*(1), 28–36.

Meyer, R. L. (2002). The demand for flexible microfinance products: Lessons from Bangladesh. *Journal of International Development, 14*(3), 351–368.

MicroMeter, 31 March 2020, Issue 33, Microfinance Institutions Network. www.mfinindia.org.

MFIN. (2016). *Microfinance Institutions Network.* www.mfinindia.org.

Mookherjee, D., & Motta, A. (2016). A theory of interactions between MFIs and informal lenders. *Journal of Development Economics, 121,* 191–200.

Nair, T. S. (2010). Commercial microfinance and social responsibility: A critique. *Economic and Political Weekly,* 32–37.

Navin, N., & Sinha, P. (2019). Market structure and competition in the Indian microfinance sector. *Vikalpa, 44*(4), 167–181.

Rhyne, E. (2002). Surviving the crisis: Microfinance in Bolivia, 1999–2002. *ACCION mimeo* for Symposium on Financial Sector Development in Southeast Europe, Kreditanstalt für Wiederaufbau.

Sriram, M. (2016). *Inclusive finance India report 2016.* Sage.

Unsworth, S., & Williams, G. (2011). Using political economy analysis to improve EU development effectiveness. *A DEVCO Concept Paper, Final Draft.*

Van Tassel, E. (2014). *Microfinance loan portfolios and external subsidies.*

Whitfield, L., & Therkildsen, O. (2011). *What drives states to support the development of productive sectors? Strategies ruling elites pursue for political survival and their policy implications* (No. 2011: 15). DIIS working paper.

World Bank. (2008). *The political economy of policy reform: Issues and implications for policy dialogue and development operations*. World Bank.

Yanguas, P., & Hulme, D. (2014). *Can aid bureaucracies think politically? The administrative challenges of political economy analysis (PEA) in DFID and the World Bank.*

Zingales, L., & Rajan, R. G. (2003). *Banks and markets: The changing character of European finance* (No. w9595). National Bureau of Economic Research.

CHAPTER 6

Role of Government in Inclusive Banking in India

The political economy perspective moots that the government's role is important to bind various constituents of inclusive finance edifice. Donors and investors will be motivated to finance MFIs only if the institutions act in consonance with the government's policies. Since the pressure groups and short-term populist agenda influences the policy, its long-term efficacy needs to be examined with a balanced rational approach.

This chapter provides an overview of the financial inclusion objective in the macroeconomic policy space in India. It discusses the debate on bringing the state in the inclusive finance space. State intervention has federal finance dimensions. The chapter delves into the challenges of centre-state coordination in inclusive finance. Lastly, the related question of whether the inclusive banking policy should be centralized or localized is addressed.

Macroeconomic Goal of Poverty Reduction and Social Justice

Poverty reduction and social justice are the macroeconomic goals of Indian Government. In the current context, social justice is defined as an equal opportunity for all to earn income.

The macroeconomic policy in independent India emphasized the top-down approach by believing that industrial growth would percolate to

L. Kulkarni and V. C. Joshi, *Inclusive Banking In India*,
https://doi.org/10.1007/978-981-33-6797-5_6

the masses. During the 1970s, the limitations of this strategy of planned industrialization were evident in the form of widespread poverty and unbalanced growth. The rising concern that the benefits of economic growth were distributed inequitably led to a shift in macroeconomic policy from industrialization for growth to inclusive growth as a strategy for poverty reduction.

Inclusive growth implies economic growth with equal opportunities for all individuals for access to better well-being. The equality of opportunity should encompass the poor and economically vulnerable and the excluded in availing the fruits of economic growth of a country. This kind of inclusive growth has positive externalities and brings benefits to the entire society. According to the erstwhile Planning Commission of India, the concept 'Inclusion' is a process of including the excluded whose participation is essential in the development process, and not simply as welfare targets of development programmes (Planning Commission, 2007). The Eleventh Five-Year Plan (2007–2012) envisioned inclusive growth as a key policy objective.

The government's programmes of financial inclusion have always been implemented through banks. It relies on the public sector banks for implementation of financial inclusion.

K. C. Chakravarty (2009) has classified the process of financial inclusion in India into three phases. In the first phase (1960–1990), the policy of subsidized credit to the priority sectors through the banks and the government's initiatives was adopted. During the second phase (1990–2005), the policy focus was on building institutional framework through reforms. The linkage between formal and informal institutions in financial inclusion arena was emphasized through SHG-bank-linkage programme and Kisan Credit Cards (KCCs) for providing credit to farmers. During the third phase (2005 onwards), the financial inclusion was explicitly made a policy objective and the thrust was on providing safe facility of savings deposits through no frills accounts. This policy was continued after 2013 in the form of PMJDY accounts.

Figure 6.1 summarizes these phases of government policy and includes the latest phase of universalization of financial services through the government initiatives of PMJDY, PMMY and Aadhaar.

From the nationalization of banks in 1969 until the ongoing phase of implementation of PMJDY in 2014, banks had the responsibility of managing the supply side obstacles that prevent poor and disadvantaged social groups from gaining access to the financial system.

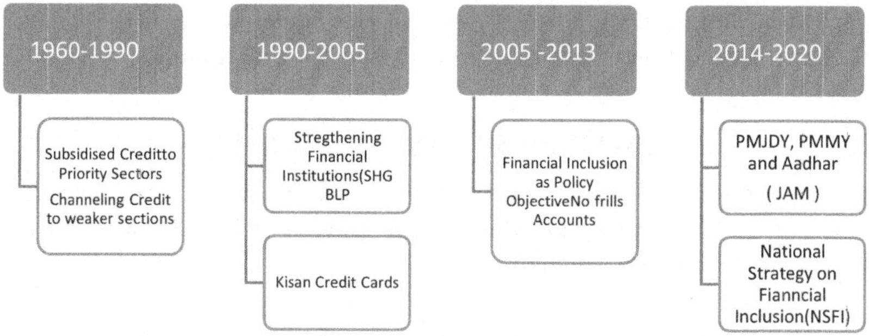

Fig. 6.1 Phases of Government Policy on Inclusive Finance in India (*Source* Based on Chakrabarty, 2009)

The macroeconomic policy also influences the demand-side factors which are essential for access to finance to the poor. These factors are the availability of collateral and reliable sources of income and wealth. In the absence of these factors, the poor cannot participate in the financial markets to borrow and thus have to depend on the informal sector for credit for their consumption needs as well as to make use of growth opportunities. The demand-side factors can be removed only in the long run with the macroeconomic policy of equitable growth.

Since 2013 India has been experimenting with universalization of financial services. JAM aimed to provide access to entire gamut of financial services from bank accounts to pensions at affordable costs to the poor. Every beneficiary needs a bank account. At the time of COVID-19 pandemic, the government schemes of direct benefit transfer (DBT) have presumed that every needy person has a bank account. JAM, trinity implemented since 2014, is expected to achieve this.

In most of the states, the DBT has propelled the usage of Jan Dhan Accounts by the poor. In many cases, the accounts are being credited and used for the first time ever and the banks faced challenges of reviving the inactive accounts. Pandemic relief schemes in the form of DBT have highlighted lacuna in the implementation of government schemes. The migrant workers, informal sector labourers and floating population of seasonal workers have still not opened the Aadhaar and Jan Dhan accounts perhaps for want of documentation. People at the margin and below subsistence levels do not have the need and motivation to open the

PMJDY account. They felt this need for the first time when the benefits could not reach them because of the absence of the accounts.

Challenges in Implementation

Many studies have shown success of government-sponsored programmes in countries like Kenya and others in sub-Saharan Africa. However, India faces unique challenges which are:

1. Geographical expanse: Schemes like PMJDY have been largely successful but some areas remain uncovered. It is challenging to reach out to every nook and corner of the country but with persistent efforts it should be possible.
2. Crippling regional disparity: It hampers the access to finance. The urban-rural divide is acute in some states and districts. According to the CRISIL Inclusix Report (2018), the average CRISIL Inclusix score of bottom 50 districts in India is 20.5 against the national score of 58.0. The top 10 districts with high CRISIL Inclusix score contained only 24% of the total population.
3. Seasonal domestic migrants: The government's schemes have been successful in covering the targeted population. However, the floating population due to seasonal/ad hoc/shifting jobs in the informal sector is not entirely covered. In a field survey of 100 slum dwellers conducted by us in Pune, 23 were unbanked and approximately 40 did not use any form of cashless transaction. Most of them were informal sector migrant labourers. The studies on financial inclusion policies for the migrants are needed.
4. Centre-state dichotomy: Effective implementation of the government's schemes depends on the ruling parties at the centre and states. If the ruling party at the state is the same as that at the centre, a scheme launched by the central government is closely monitored and effectively implemented, otherwise not.
5. Operational lags and lack of ownership: Government's schemes are well designed on paper but the implementation requires motivated agencies with goal-driven people to implement them. Success at the ground level ultimately depends on the local political leaders, community group leaders and their motivational power. Hence, in

areas where these factors are in place, the government's schemes as well as the MFI and SHG movements are successful.

A strong political will is a must to tackle these challenges. However, the links between democratic accountability and financial inclusion are not clear-cut. Delivering to the poor is characterized by a classic collective action problem where there are a large number of beneficiaries who are disorganized and lack bargaining power. As against this, a handful of elite people who can lose because of financial inclusion are organized and powerful (Haber et al., 2020).

Bringing the State in—Need for Coordination in State and Central Government Schemes

Role of the government in economic development is crucial. Economists do not have a consensus on this subject macroeconomic thought is preoccupied with determining whether the state intervention makes or mars the economy. Since World War II, welfare economics, Keynesianism and the early development economics interventionist theories have been arguing that active state intervention is necessary to correct market failures.

In India, the Government at the central and state levels has been active in inclusive finance policy. Since 2013–2014, the role of the government's schemes in financial inclusion has become more prominent.

Flagship Government Schemes for Financial Inclusion

Many studies and reports address the features, success and failures of government schemes. Here we provide an overview of the features and address selected limitations from viewpoint of commercial banks.

In August 2014, the National Mission for Financial Inclusion (NMFI) was launched with the aim of covering every household under the universal financial inclusion drive. The PMJDY mission aimed at opening bank accounts of 100% population in India.

PMJDY as a Product—Panacea for Banking the Unbanked

The scheme has been appreciated for its drive for financial inclusion.

Its main features are:

1. **Basic account**: It can be opened with a small sum or zero deposit with minimum documentation.
2. **Easy access**: Subserved areas in villages were identified across India. In areas without bank branches, agents named Bank Mitras were appointed to provide access to banking.
3. **Cashless facility**: PMJDY facilitates cashless banking through debit cards.
4. **Insurance cover**: The financial inclusion initiative covers other services like insurance with inbuilt accident insurance cover of Rs. 2 lakhs and access to overdraft facility.
5. **Inclusion in insurance and pension**: It aims at universalization of social security at a broader level. Various schemes like health insurance (Pradhan Mantri Suraksha Bima Yojana), life insurance (Pradhan Mantri Jeevan Jyoti Bima Yojana) and guaranteed minimum pension (Atal Pension Yojana) are also launched.

   Thus, on paper it is almost a dream scheme. Still the data from the Global Findex (2017) report as well as a number of local studies show that it has not achieved full coverage of bankable population during last five years.

Successful in Coverage

According to the data published at PMJDY website, the scheme has achieved its targets by opening accounts of 40.35 crore beneficiaries. According to the reported data, 60% of the PMJDY accounts are opened in rural areas and 53% account holders are women. This scheme has helped to implement fiscal direct benefit package during the pandemic when the amount of cash benefits was credited directly to the women members' accounts. The deposit base of PMJDY accounts has expanded over time. As on March 27, 2019, the deposits in PMJDY accounts totalled Rs. 96,107 crores. The average deposit per account has more than doubled from Rs. 1,064 in March 2015 to Rs. 2,725 in March 2019.

- The Bank Mitras network has gained in strength and usage. The average number of transactions per Bank Mitra on the Aadhaar Enabled Payment System operated by Bank Mitras has risen by over 80-fold from 52 transactions in 2014–2015 to 4,291 transactions in 2016–2017.

Other Initiatives by Government

Along with the PMJDY, schemes like Pradhan Mantri Mudra Yojana (PMMY) for microlending to the young, educated or skilled workers who aspire to become first-generation entrepreneurs and also existing small businesses was launched. However, it was not successful.

In addition, a whole gamut of schemes like Pradhan Mantri Suraksha Bima Yojana (PMSBY), an accidental death and disability insurance scheme;

Atal Pension Yojana (APY) to provide social security during old age; and

Pradhan Mantri Vaya Vandana Yojana were launched by the Central Government. These schemes are for those who have bank accounts and Aadhaar cards.

Public Sector Banks Mandated to Implement the Schemes

The government relies completely on public sector banks for the implementation of these schemes.

The National Strategy for Financial Inclusion Report (NSFI, 2019) explicitly mentions that RBI has adopted a bank-led model to deepen financial inclusion. This approach has been adopted right from the initiation of financial inclusion by nationalizing the banks in 1969.

The government's financial inclusion drive has been implemented through the state-owned banks for decades. From 1990 to 2000s, banks were required to open branches and ATMs in unbanked areas throughout India. Since 2012, they are required to prepare financial inclusion plans (FIPs).

According to the recommendations of the Mohanty Committee on Financial Inclusion under chairmanship of Dr.Deepak Mohanty, a Financial Inclusion Fund (FIF) was created for training for technology adoption for financial inclusion. In 2015, differential banking licence and payment banks have been experimented.

Narasimham Committee and academicians raised concerns over using banking system for providing subsidized finance to the poor. They were regarding the effects on public sector banks' profitability, bank autonomy (Banerjee et al., 2004; Basu, 2005; Deokar & Shetty, 2013).

The 2017 Global Findex Data shows that India had significantly improved financial inclusion over the past four years. According to it, the bank account ownership increased from 53% of the population owning accounts in 2014 to 80% in 2017. The latest Findex and FII surveys agree that PMJDY has been the principal means of increases in financial inclusion since 2014 (Raman, 2018).

Reliance on Banks Has Not Decreased in Spite of Academic Criticism

All the government schemes depend on the banking network in India. The mandate regarding the modalities of the schemes is determined by the government and RBI and the schemes are to be implemented by the commercial banks.

For instance, the mandate from the finance ministry is to open a branch within 15 km radius of a village where there are no banking facilities. Under branch expansion drive, the branch opening has to be as per the locations provided by the ministry (*The Economic Times*, January 17, 2020). Large public sector banks have to open nearly 1,500 branches in villages and panchayat regions where there are no bank branches to push cheap credit to the unbanked areas.

The policy of branch expansion and targeting number of accounts newly opened has certain limitations which are documented in three reports based on various parameters to measure financial inclusion. The Global Findex Report 2017 provides a Financial Inclusion Index (FII) measures financial inclusion based on access and usage of accounts, CRISIL provides Inclusix index focusing on regional financial inclusion in India and the recent Boston Consultancy Group Index focuses on the sustainability of financial inclusion along with access and usage.

These reports point out the following gaps in India's achievements as regards financial inclusion:

Low Usage of Accounts: The Global Findex Report, 2018 stated that though India has 80% of the population owning bank accounts, 48% of the bank accounts are inactive. The Findex (2017) and Intermedia's 2018 Financial Inclusion Insights (FII) survey (FII) reports both opine that accounts use is low because so many accounts are recent but that the usage is likely to increase over time (Raman 2018).

Gender Parity Still to Be Achieved

FII data states that the account ownership for women has increased in India. Just 39 per cent of them had accounts in 2013 in contrast to 76 per cent in 2017. This has helped a number of women account holders at the time of government pandemic relief by way of direct benefit transfers to them.

Need for Newer Multidimensional Parameters of Financial Inclusion

The entire focus of the inclusive banking policy so far has been on, expansion of bank network, and increase in bank account ownership. The policy needs to change its emphasis on branch expansion. The strategy of branch expansion now becomes less effective as the branchless banking is possible with the new electronic technology. Thus, the role of the regulator and the government should now be shifted from directing mandatory financial inclusion strategies implemented through public sector banks to building Fintech infrastructure facilitating environment to motivate the banks to adopt the underprivileged clientele in their business model. As shown by the reports (Findex, 2017), account ownership on paper does not ensure use and sustained inclusion in mainstream finance. To achieve them, the banks and the policymakers have to work together and the banks must perceive the unbanked segment as their potential customer for a long business association. The targets of the schemes should change accordingly.

Sustaining the Financial Inclusion Is a Global Challenge

The Boston Consulting Group (BCG) has developed qualitative and quantitative measures to capture financial inclusion. They are set out to capture financial inclusion in three parameters. First is the financial services, transactions, credit, accounts and insurance. Secondly, it measures usage. The third and most important measure is of sustainability of financial inclusion.

According to the Boston Consultancy Group, report (2017), no country has solved the financial inclusion puzzle. Even the most economically developed and financially inclusive countries such as Australia and France do not come up all green in the sustainable-financial-inclusion framework. In other words, there is work to be done in all the countries.

Centralized Approach vs. Localized Approach

In India, the functions of the central government and state governments are bifurcated in three lists, viz., Union List, State List and Concurrent or Joint List. Finance is not exclusively in the Union List. Financial inclusion and regulation is a central government subject but micro-finance is a state government subject. Some issues become more complex as commercial banks are a central government subject. Hence, loan recovery rules are governed by the RBI. However, the state and local governance gets involved in foreclosure of default assets. But these have been a result of expediency rather than a well-thought out strategy. Financial inclusion is not specifically mentioned in any of these lists. The Microfinance Bill, 2012 made RBI the regulator for microfinance. In this sense, the microfinance sector comes under the purview of the central government.

States are probably disinterested in demanding more power in financial inclusion. Financial inclusion is not a topic of conflict as they might be perceiving it as a responsibility and item of expenditure rather than revenue. State governments are motivated to ask for grants and subsidies from the centre because they have a short-term visible effect. This is a typical case of time inconsistency problem in fiscal expenditure policy.

In the federal system, the issue is whether financial inclusion should be a responsibility of the central government or states' prerogative. In India currently the central government and the RBI undertake the responsibility of strategy for financial inclusion and the implementation is left to the state and local governments. Centralization in policy making has some disadvantages like complexity, lack of accountability, sluggish implementation and low response by states with a different ruling party than that at the centre. When the schemes are formulated at the central level, the policymakers often lose touch with the local level problems. Hence, centralization in policymaking should be encouraged judiciously to enhance the effectiveness of the policy.

On the other hand, localization is not a perfect way. The local governments are driven by the populist ways to get immediate gratification and credit for financing the poor. There emerge cases of frauds, nepotism and misappropriation of funds at local level. In financial sector many a time local level companies, frauds, Ponzi schemes, etc., are better handled by the state governments as they have knowledge of the regional issues and command over the related agencies.

Road Ahead

The government's effort at financial inclusion would be fully successful only if the Government brings the banks in the picture. Policies of microlending and deposit mobilization by banks are not standalone solutions to include the underprivileged and improve their lives. The cooperation between various agencies is necessary. This can be achieved by bringing in the local agricultural universities. Agencies in a local area should come together to achieve all this.

A cursory glance at these schemes reflects the maximum extent to which the benefit should have accrued. The return on investment on all these initiatives has been negligible taking into account the system costs. Many a time the loans are given to meet the targets. One must realize that just an increase in the number of accounts and amount of microloans is not going to make a real difference in the lives of those who are currently excluded and underprivileged. One cannot expect a poor individual to become an entrepreneur overnight and be successful in his micro-enterprise. Many of the micro-enterprises are financially not viable and hardly meet the costs. In their work *Poor Economics*, Banerjee and Dufflo (2011, p. 217) provide an example of the accounts of a typical petty shop to bring out this fact. Generally, the scale of microlending is too small to establish any worthwhile sustainable business. For example, a loan for a cow or a couple goats is not going to propel a poor household into entrepreneurial prosperity. Micro-enterprises with these small loans are petty shops. However, the partially literate borrowers do not know the nuances of business or accounting. Most of the times women members of the SHGs borrow only for urgent consumption needs, medical emergencies, education of their children, etc.[1] The policies should bring together all agencies along with the banks to make the financed units viable so that the financial inclusion becomes sustainable for the beneficiaries as well as for the banks. The way out is to bring about a collaborative endeavour among all the parties and try to develop economic activities which are viable and sustainable.

In his book titled *Kicking Away the Ladder* (2002), Ha-Joon Chang discusses the role of government in the developed countries (or what he terms as 'the now-developed' countries). As far as the role of the government in economic development is concerned, what lessons

[1] Findings from a field survey of SHGs in South India by authors (2019).

today's developing countries can learn from the experiences of the 'now-developed' countries? He shows that the now-developed countries relied on the interventionist policies to achieve economic growth. Their governments played an important role while their institutional infrastructure was weak. However, as Chang points out, the governments in today's developing countries are less protectionist. These countries have better institutions, like central banks and financial institutions, than the now-developed countries had at comparable stages of development in eighteenth and nineteenth centuries. Thus, he argues that to achieve the desired economic growth, today's developing countries have to encourage a framework *that kicks away the ladder* of protectionism and interventionist policies. In the Indian context, the banking and financial sector provides a promise that if a pragmatic futuristic strategy is adopted, it is possible that the sector itself can take up the responsibility of providing access to finance to the poor by bringing them into the mainstream financial system. Bringing the less privileged into the mainstream financial sector will help in minimizing the reliance on the government to achieve financial inclusion as the banking sector would be able to integrate the poor clientele in its commercial business model.

References

Banerjee, A. V., & Duflo, E. (2011). *Poor economics: Rethinking poverty & the ways to end it*. Random House India.

Banerjee, A., Cole, S., & Duflo, E. (2004, June). Banking reform in India. In *India policy forum* (Vol. 1, No. 1, pp. 277–332). Global Economy and Development Program, The Brookings Institution.

Basu, P. (2005). A financial system for India's poor. *Economic and Political Weekly*, 4008–4012.

Chang, H. J. (2002). *Kicking away the ladder: Development strategy in historical perspective*. Anthem Press.

Chakrabarty, Dr. K. C. (2009). The Address delivered by Deputy Governor, Reserve Bank of India at the Mint's 'Clarity Through Debate' series on August 10th, 2009 at Chennai. https://rbidocs.rbi.org.in/rdocs/Speeches/PDFs/DSPC130809.pdf.

Choudhury, D. (2013, July 10). *Centre-state relations in the world of financial policy, The Live Mint*. https://www.livemint.com/Opinion/djJJ4x7r561LyahCykyeTM/Centrestate-relations-in-the-world-of-financial-policy.html.

CRISIL Inclusix Report. (2018). *Financial inclusion surges, driven by Jan-Dhan Yojana*. https://www.crisil.com/content/dam/crisil/our-analysis/reports/

Research/documents/2018/march/crisil-inclusix-financial-inclusion-surges-driven-by-Jan-Dhan-yojana.pdf.

Demirgüç-Kunt, A., Leora, K., Dorothe, S., Saniya, A., & Jake, H. (2018). *The Global Findex Database 2017: Measuring Financial Inclusion and the Fintech Revolution.* World Bank. https://doi.org/10.1596/978-1-4648-1259-0. License: Creative Commons Attribution CC BY 3.0 IGO.

Deokar, B., & Shetty, S. (2013). Priority sector credit: Disappointments after the Nair committee report. *Economic and Political Weekly,* 55–57.

Haber, S., Frieden, J., Levine, R., Maurer, N., Robinson, J., Hoffs, G., & Sokoloff, K. (2020). *Political competition and economic growth: Lessons from the political economy of banking in Mexico and the United States.*

Boston Consultancy Group Report. (2017). Ikdal, A, Naidoo, E., Portafaix, A., Hendrickson, J., Boje, A., Rabec, D., & Kessler, K. (2017). *How to create and sustain financial inclusion BCG analysis.* https://www.bcg.com/publications/2017/globalization-how-create-sustain-financial-inclusion.

Intermedia Financial Inclusion Insight Report. (2018). http://finclusion.org/country/asia/india.html#dataAtAGlance.

Narasimham, M. (1991). *Report of the committee on the financial system.* Bella Vista.

Planning Commission. (2007). *Government of India, 11th Five Year Plan 2007–2012, Inclusive Growth Vol. I.* https://niti.gov.in/planningcommission.gov.in/docs/plans/planrel/fiveyr/11th/11_v1/11th_vol1.pdf.

Raman A. (2018, August 30). *India moves toward universal financial inclusion* (CGAP Blog) https://www.cgap.org/blog/india-moves-toward-universal-financial-inclusion.

RBI. (2019). *National strategy for financial inclusion 2019–2024 report.* https://rbidocs.rbi.org.in/rdocs/content/pdfs/NSFIREPORT100119.pdf.

Shukla, S. (2020, January 17). *The Economic Times, Govt asks banks to open 15,000 branches in FY21.* https://economictimes.indiatimes.com/industry/banking/finance/banking/govt-asks-banks-to-open-15000-branches-in-fy21/articleshow/73286116.cms?from=mdr.

CHAPTER 7

New Developments in Inclusive Finance

This chapter delves into four developments in the social and inclusive finance sector in India, i.e. (i) digital revolution in inclusive finance sector, (ii) launching of social stock exchange in India, (iii) microenterprise collaboratives and (iv) conversion of MFIs into the banks.

Launching of Social Equity Market is the newest of these developments. The idea of social enterprises raising funds from the capital markets offers various possibilities for the future of the sector. All these developments like digitalization, participatory collaboratives and social equity market do have a potential to provide solutions for specific problems faced by inclusive banking. It is often reported that banks make half-hearted effort at including the poor clientele in their customer base because of high operating costs and hard to monitor small loans. Digitalization and data revolution can provide solutions to this problem. Similarly, studies always mention that microlending alone would not be sufficient to turn the poor into businessmen (Banerjee & Duflo, 2011). The participatory microenterprise collaboratives could be explored as an answer to this issue.

Digitalization and New Development Possibilities in Inclusive Finance

India is a hub of technology and digital services to the world. New advances in financial technology offer unthinkable potential for progress

L. Kulkarni and V. C. Joshi, *Inclusive Banking In India*,
https://doi.org/10.1007/978-981-33-6797-5_7

in all spheres of life. According to an analysis by Accenture, investment in the Fintech sector in India has shown a 100% rise from $1.9 billion in 2018 to $3.7 billion in 2019 (Bhatia, 2020, *Moneycontrol News*, Feb. 24, 2020). This pegs the country as the world's third largest Fintech centre, trailing behind the USA and UK. This potential can also be used effectively in the inclusive finance field to remove the obstacles in access to finance and banking to the underprivileged masses.

As discussed earlier, the all-pervasive network of banks has been only half-heartedly implementing the financial inclusion initiatives as they consider it to be financially non-viable. Microlending business becomes non-viable because of high operating costs and hard to monitor clientele. Financial technology (Fintech) emerges as an opportunity to eliminate these impediments to microlending. Banks can be motivated to implement the inclusive financial products like zero-balance accounts and they can find that microlending can turn out to be their core business.

According to Arner et al. (2015), use of financial technology can range from QR codes that enable cashless payment through digital platforms that could connect lenders and borrowers to digital lending. At present, there are 144 Fintech companies that have been registered with the Financial Services Authority, up from just 32 in January 2018.

International community has agreed that the future of financial inclusion is through Fintech revolution. Some countries like Kenya (M-Pesa) and Vietnam have successfully used technology, mobile banking, for effective financial inclusion (BIS, 2020a, b).

Technology and innovation have a key role in payment transactions and financial inclusion if the risks are well managed.

The outlook of Fintech in India is bright even after the pandemic. The government is also encouraging the Fintech revolution with a vision of digital India financial inclusion to be achieved through mobile banking.

After the demonetization in 2016, the cashless transactions drive, new Aadhaar enabled payments systems and *Bhim*, UPI has expanded in the urban areas. More than 80% of the urban population is using digital transactions.

Fintech Industry Finds Synergy in Rural Outreach

Reports estimate the number of smartphone users in India at approximately 900 million. The use of Internet and mobiles in rural India is also increasing at a phenomenal rate PwC—ASSOCHAM joint study (2019) and investors are aware of this potential market. The vision of cashless revolution for financial inclusion can only be realized if the products are made easier to understand and are designed for the local user in rural areas with customized features like local language apps.

Due to e-commerce, entrepreneurship and self-employment in semi-urban and rural areas are also encouraged (Lee, 2019). Deloitte Report on Fintech in India (July 2017) depicts the stages of Fintech revolution. Four layers of advancement of Fintech revolution are visualized as taking place in four consecutive stages. These stages are (i) collection of data in consent layer, (ii) use of cashless transactions in cashless layer, (iii) paperless transactions in lending borrowing in paperless layer and (iv) presence of less financial services in the presence less layer. The journey from cashless to presence less finance would not be far in the future given the speed of advancements in financial technology. At least a part of these developments would facilitate the newer business models by the banks to expand outreach of lending to the poor by removing current impediments as shown in Fig. 7.1 above.

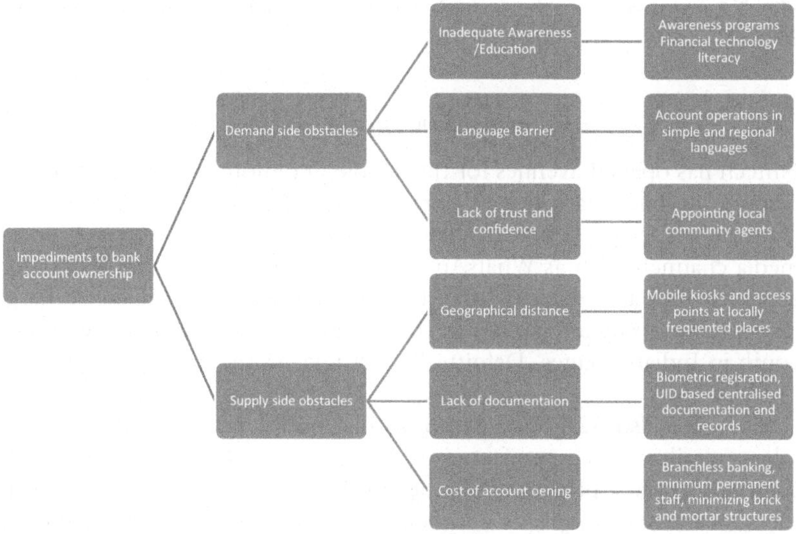

Fig. 7.1 Impediments to bank account ownership and possible measure (*Source* Compiled by the authors)

Structure

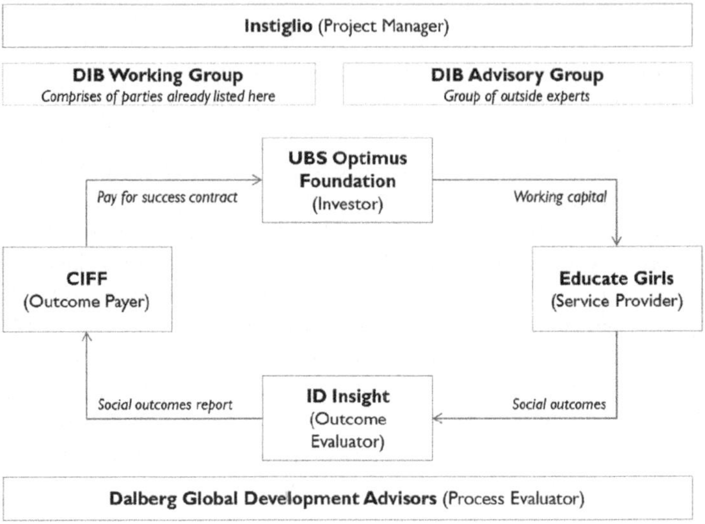

Fig. 7.2 Structure of educate girls social impact bond (*Source* Instiglio, May 2015)

Creating New Income Avenues

Fintech has opened avenues for the people in remote areas to earn money through mobile smartphones. For example, *Meesho* is a social commerce platform. It helps people to launch online businesses through social media channels such as WhatsApp, Facebook and Instagram. Many 'gig' economy jobs are emerging, e.g. helping people in their village recharge their phones using an app is a freelance earning source of many educated youth in Indian villages. Deloitte Report reviews the potential of Fintech in India.

There are also B2B trade platforms that bring together traders, wholesalers, retailers and manufacturers. For instance, *Udaan* is a network-centric B2B trade platform, helping small and medium traders to expand their businesses. Shopix is another e-venture helping intermediaries to connect with direct manufacturers of products.

Financial Awareness Trainings

Like banks, Fintech companies also initiate financial awareness programmes. These programmes help poor clientele to understand the digital payment services to encourage their use. In countries like India, customizing the digital/mobile services with regional languages is essential to facilitate their use. These developments have great potential for expanding inclusive banking in remote regions.

Fintech for Uplifting the Poor in Specific Segments

Some Fintech firms work in specific segments of consumers. One wallet has launched Paper King platform for newspaper sellers. It has over 5000 newspaper vendors on its platform and processes to Rs. 4 crores of bill generation every month. To expand the use of technology in transactions, the government should make efforts to increase financial literacy.

In the current times, the gig economy is expanding with many youngsters and self-employed people working as freelancers and contractual workers. This segment remains excluded as far as formal bank lending is concerned. Bon is a digital lending start-up that provides micro-credit for this sector. It lends to a wide range of temporary/ad hoc/freelance professionals like radio taxi drivers, freelance writers/data scientists and Swiggy contract workers. Because of their variable earnings, they do not have a credit score, thus excluding them from formal bank lending. Out of its current 25,000 borrowers, three-fourths did not have access to credit (MEDICI, 2019).

Jai Kisan, a Fintech start-up, provides easy, cheap and quick lending for farmers for their productive activities.

Gaps in Outreach

Although Fintech is making headways in inclusive finance, there is still a lot to be accomplished. While stakeholders are making efforts to push digital payments, less than 2% merchants have made cashless payments till date.

India FinTech Report 2019 classifies the Indian economy on the basis of levels of financial empowerment through digitalization. 'India 1' segment is the $9000 per head income population that is approx. 110 million people owning 1 trillion of GDP. The high-stake payment and trading digital platforms like razorpay, zerodha, etc., cater to this segment, the middle segment with an average per head income of $3000 is using the payment apps by companies like PhonePe, Paytm, etc., while the bottom segment with 1126 million Indians is addressed by the fintech. There are few companies like Jai Kisan, Bon and One Wallet but a huge gap still remains to be bridged. The report mentions that Fintech should now serve India 3 segment (Mishra, 2019). It enlists preconditions for the Fintech companies to reach the last mile. They can be summarized as financial literacy, ground-level studies to provide customized products and services, and involvement of young minds in the incubation of new ideas for financial inclusion. Inclusive banking with strategic partnership between the banks and Fintech firms is indispensable for the success of digital financial inclusion. Greater use of technology by microfinance institutions is necessary as the overall picture at the ground level reflects that apart from the use of computers, technology is not used in the microfinance arena. The report also calls for the government's intervention to provide the necessary Internet infrastructure, regulatory framework and launch of special portals for SMEs, etc.

Keeping up with the Technology Advancements

Banks have to move speedily and adapt the financial technology. The report by Saal et al. (2017) classified the countries into four quadrants based on the progress of banking outreach and technological progress. India falls in the Quadrant III (Lower Right) where 'Tech Dominance' countries are characterized by an advanced technological ecosystem but a large segment of the population is excluded from banking, creating a business potential for the Fintech companies to tap this market segment.

Capital Market for Social Sector Enterprises

A comparatively lesser known and contentious alternative channel of funding inclusive finance is through the capital markets. According to the Brookings India study titled *The Promise of Impact Investing in India* (Ravi et al., 2019, p. 9), in a survey of Indian social enterprises, 57% identified access to debt or equity as a barrier to growth and sustainability.

The need to tap the markets for financing needs of social enterprises has led to the evolution of the idea of social capital markets. This has been felt at the global level due to ever-growing paucity of funding for social enterprises.

Internationally funding by donor agencies is growing at a moderate speed (OECD, 2016) Reports also predict constrained development finance with regime changes at various levels across the globe (Oroxom et al., 2018).

Social enterprises need a different kind of equity market to suit their needs and stick to their values. The social stock exchange aims to provide a new model of raising funds for social enterprises by issuing public offerings to a larger public in the stock market.

Social Stock Exchange in India

Regulators and policy-makers expect that banks and institutions should finance their own social sector endeavours. In this scenario, funding for social ventures can be raised from the capital markets through social investment instruments. With the recent wash-down of businesses after the pandemic, the flow of funds through corporate social responsibility (CSR) also will be affected. Hence, social sector institutions can explore new avenues of funding through capital markets. This concept is prevalent globally in various versions. Countries like the UK, Canada and Brazil have SSEs. In India in the Union Budget speech in 2019, the finance minister announced launching of the social equity market. In 2016, the first social impact bond was floated in the Educate Girls project in Rajasthan. This concept will now gain momentum in India with the government's support and regulatory institutional framework. A report on the Social Stock Exchange in India was published by a working group constituted by SEBI in September 2019 under the chairmanship of Ishaat Hussain, Director at SBI Foundation and former finance director in Tata Sons.

As of now this is the only official document describing the stand of the government and the regulator on the Social Stock Exchange in India.

According to the draft SEBI report (June 2020), a Social Stock Exchange (SSEs) may be helpful in rebuilding the livelihood of people who are affected during pandemics like COVID-19.

1. Trading on Stock Exchange—An SSE allows the listing of non-profit or non-government organizations on stock exchanges, providing

them with an alternative fund-raising structure. It may be listed either on BSE or NSE.

2. Listing on the SSE—At this juncture, SEBI does not define a social enterprise. The report clarifies that the meaning is varied and at this stage it will be categorization is based on the self-declaration of social purpose and a proven record of social impact.
3. Instruments to be issued and traded: The report states that the listing of enterprises on the exchange will be through direct listing of bonds **in** Social Venture Funds (SVFs).

   Fund-raising is proposed through several instruments such as zero-coupon-zero-principal bonds, social venture funds and mutual funds. The duration of listing of an entity depends on its objectives and future plans.

   According to the SEBI's, *Report of Working Group on Social Stock Exchange* (June 2020), the objectives of eth social stock exchange in India can be summarized as follows:

   1. expanding the range of listed instruments for providing capital to social enterprises with maintaining, reporting, auditing and accounting standards.
   2. The instruments at the exchange will add to the existing sources of funds to the social enterprises and not discard any existing source.
   3. The committee recommends inclusive approach of allowing participation by the smallest of the NGOs irrespective of size or scale of operations.

      Accommodating NPOs/NGOs of diverse scales and sizes—India has over 31 lakh NPOs (Sharma, 2020). A majority of NPOs are small and the principle of equity is an important consideration. Lack of Investment readiness and small scale of the non-profit organizations is considered.

4. The committee recommended Social Venture Fund (SVF) for pooling of small non-profit organizations.

Another form of social capital market is the market for social impact bonds (SIBs). After the first SIB in the UK, they are gradually being experimented with in other countries (Culley, 2011; Disley et al., 2011; Fraser et al., 2018). The USA has 17 social impact bonds in different areas of social enterprises. In India, the first social impact bond was launched in 2014 which matured in 2018 and was a great success.

India's Experiment with Social Impact Bonds

The following discussion is based on the Report on Evaluation of Educate Girls Social Impact Bond (EducateGirls Report, 2018).

The Case of Primary Education Initiative by 'Educate Girls' in Rajasthan

The world's second development impact bond (DIB) and India's first was launched in 2014. Its purpose was to finance the initiative by Educate Girls, an NGO, to increase the enrolment of girls in primary schools in Rajasthan. The second objective was to improve learning outcomes of 18,000 primary school children. This bond is called the 'Educate Girls DIB' (Instiglio, 2015) (Fig. 7.2).

The NGO received funding from UBS Optimus for implementing this intervention during a span of three years. Another firm IDinsight acted as an evaluator to examine the outcomes achieved by the NGO. In 2018, the bond matured and the IDinsight evaluated the outcomes to report the involved counterparties viz., CIFF, UBS Optimus and Educate Girls. CIFF then paid to UBS Optimus. UBS invested USD 238,000 for service provision in the project.

The outcome was an improvement in the girls' primary education. The social impact bond return is the social impact achieved by the receiving organization. Social impact being a qualitative variable has to be translated into a social impact matrix for evaluation. In this case, the IDinsight acted as the consultant for designing the bond and monitoring and evaluating the results. The social impact outcomes specified at the launch of the bond were 80% of the total outcome payment. On improvement in learning of children in classes 3–5 and the remaining 20% of the payment on increase in enrolment of girls of age 7–14 in classes from 2nd standard to 8th standard in school (Instiglio, 2015).

Success of the First Social Impact Bond in India

The performance of the bond is evaluated each year in terms of the specified outcome matrix. This first DIB was successful in achieving greater outcomes than expected.

Based on this encouraging result, of the first experiment, now India has two more social impact bonds.

The second social impact bond was launched in September 2017. This is a Humanitarian Impact Bond (HIB) as the outcomes are improvising humanitarian issues like physical rehabilitation.

Another development impact bond was launched in December 2017. The Population Services International (PSI) and Hindustan Latex Family Planning Promotion Trust (HLFPPT) launched a bond for improving maternal and newborn health in Rajasthan. Various agencies involved in the design and implementation of this bond are the United States Agency for International Development (USAID), Merck for Mothers, UBS Optimus Foundation and Palladium.

Challenges for Social Equity and Bond Markets

The union of social sector and capital markets is regarded as a mismatch in many quarters and policy-makers. The concerns are:

1. **Complexity of measuring social outcomes:** Returns to social capital market bonds or funds are based on social outcomes. The measurement of social outcomes is extremely complex. Thus, assessment of the achievement of outcomes is tedious and unreliable. Most of the times the outcomes cannot be captured by point in time static measures but are observed across the time. Since, well-tested indicators of outcomes are not available, performance of social impact bonds remains a complex issue and can lead to disputes as the financial investments are linked to performance (McHugh et al., 2013). It is difficult to document evidence that the outcomes are attributed to a specific policy action (Arvidson et al., 2013; Pawson, 2004).

   Many studies are pessimistic about the success of social impact bonds as social policies cannot be designed around mechanically configured outcomes with each initiative involving a complex mix of responses of stakeholders, dynamic interactions and unpredictable effects (Sanderson, 2000).

2. **High costs of designing the instruments and their operation:** SIB transactions are expensive because each deal is a unique and complex negotiation (Maier et al., 2018; Warner, 2013).
3. **Appeasing the investors:** Generally, NGOs are concerned about entering the market because they fear that they would have to play to the tunes of the investors looking for profiteering and would have to artificially window dress the results in measurable monetary terms (Heinrich & Choi, 2007; Lowe et al., 2018).
4. **Financialization of social service:** According to some studies, opposition to SIBs emerges from the aversion to monetize the results of a social venture, profiteering on social objectives and commoditizing the vulnerabilities (Chiapello & Knoll, 2020; Neyland, 2017; Warner, 2013).
5. **Skewed investment in short-term low-cost programmes:** Since SIBs inherently establish a close link between social outcomes and funding, both social enterprises and social investors may be biased towards adopting initiatives with instant simple to quantify outcomes sidelining more complex long term programmes (Lake, 2016). This generates risk of marginalizing and excluding the needy (Shortall & Warner, 2010).

These concerns are expressed by the academia (Tan et al., 2019; Tse & Warner, 2018) and social sector enterprises regarding opening up the markets. If the regulation, governance and institutional framework is in place, then social capital markets are worth a try to reduce the burden on governments.

A prerequisite for establishing a social stock market is the creation of appropriate institutional infrastructure. The SIB market involves many market participants like NGOs, consultancy firms, market makers, social investors, government bodies, etc. They are from varied sectors having different work ethics and expectations. Thus, a successful market requires transparent and well-thought-out regulatory framework. If this precondition is met, then social impact bonds can be a successful new financial asset combining profit motive of the private investor with social motive of the social sector enterprise (Bolton & Saville, 2010).

Need for Bank Representation on the Boards of MFIs

Most of the MFIs (both NBFC MFIs and NGOs) have equity capital from the banking sector. One suggestion of the authors is to include bank officials on the boards of management of the MFIs. This would facilitate the credibility of the MFIs in the markets to raise capital from the stock markets. Banks will also have some supervisory control as the capital investors in NGOs/MFIs. This will also help in the distribution of loans in a more formal way. With the advent of stock exchanges, this provision will strengthen the market position of these institutions from the viewpoint of the investors.

To summarize, the concept of social capital markets brings in a major paradigm shift in financial inclusion as well as the approach of the third sector. From the perspective of the banks, if the social investors come in the picture and if the capital market funding is widely accepted by the social sector, a large part of the funding requirements of the NGOs and NBFC MFIs will be outsourced from the social capital markets. This will reduce burden of financially supporting these institutions for the banks whose in this framework will be of underwriters. Unless an elaborate institutional infrastructure is in place and a well thought out regulatory framework is devised, a widespread use of funding from social capital market is a distant possibility.

Beyond Micro Finance—Case Studies of Women's Collaboratives

Most of the existing initiatives for inclusive development focus on the access to credit for financing women's tiny informal businesses to achieve their upward economic mobility. However, literature shows that the microlending model has marginally benefitted income improvisation, resulted in debt cycles and created survival skills (Banerjee et al., 2017; Chavan & Ram Kumar, 2002; Karnani, 2009).

In developing countries, several voluntary organizations are working on development of collaboratives to provide a 360-degree support for upliftment of the poor.

The authors have studied these initiatives to assess their potential for bringing out financial inclusion and poverty reduction. Surveys of members of women's collaboratives as well as managers and founders were conducted during May–July 2019.

- One of these selected interventions is Toehold Artisans Collaborative (TAC), implemented by Asian Centre for Entrepreneurial Initiative. (This collaborative was launched in 2000 and has been operating for almost two decades in Athani village of Karnataka).
- The second intervention used for this study is Subhaksha launched in 2015 in Chitradurga district of Karnataka. The data from this intervention was used to examine the women's entrepreneurship model at the initiation stage.

Observations from these field surveys are summarized below.

The interviews of the founders, managerial staff and beneficiaries were conducted to understand the working of the venture and the impact with respect to:

- Economic empowerment: Income, savings and assets.
- Financial parameters: Costs, daily sales, business turnover, business assets, profit and growth of profits.
- Capacity building: Support provided by the programme in terms of training, inventory, marketing and other activities.
- Entrepreneurial skills development, decision-making and involvement in management of the enterprise, future business expansion and planning.
- Upward economic mobility: Next generation's education and careers/jobs /livelihoods (in case of Toehold) improvement Social familial status of women.

ToeHold Artisans Collaborative

The ToeHold Artisans Collaborative (TAC) is a women's collaborative enterprise in Athani in Belgaum district, about 720 km from Bangalore in Karnataka. It is inhabited by about 200 families of artisans from a community with a rich legacy. The Kolhapuri leather footwear is the traditional occupation since time immemorial. It requires special skills by trained artisans who have been working in this profession for generations. However, prior to 2000 most people worked on low wages as bonded labourers in footwear factories owned by traders.

The artisan community was unorganized, facing acute poverty and looking for work in other menial jobs. In the year 2000, the ASCENT

NGO of Bangalore, organized the women's SHGs and set up Toehold Artisans' Collective. It is owned and governed by the artisans through women's SHGs engaged in the making and marketing of handcrafted leather footwear.

The cooperative has changed the face of the trade. Women and their families were organized. They were trained in marketing their products in international markets. They realized the value of their craft when they received orders from international leather boutiques. They were trained in pricing their product and using machinery for cutting leather. The artisans started getting higher price for their product a part of which is reinvested in the collaborative for further progress.

In terms of increased income, before 1999 artisans could earn a net income of

about Rs. 12–15 per pair. Today it has gone up to about Rs. 40–50 per pair,

depending on the design and material used. Earlier they were making upto three pairs a day and now they make about 6 pairs a day. They were occupied for less than 150 days and now they work for about 200 days. Hence in terms of wages alone.

they earn, on an average, about Rs. 54,000/- annually from this activity as compared.

with Rs. 6075/- prior to the intervention. Apart from this, they also receive dividend at.

the end of the year in the ratio of 40% of the profit in proportion to supplies made by.

them. About 20% of the profit goes to the SHGs and 40% is retained by TAC for business.

development.

Subhaksha

Subhaksha is a women's collaborative venture under SME OneSource Make-In-India Foundation, Section-8 Company focusses on the promotion of Rural Micro Industries Development exclusively for women, farmers and service industries for youth. SME OneSource corporate ecosystem is created to support rural industrialization under the flagship programme Re-igniting the Rural Entrepreneurship. It constitutes the identification of a trust (NGO) partner formed by young graduates at taluka level. The partners are given on-the-job training ~~and skilling~~ to carry out village/community campaigns to educate women on the importance of having micro industries and the necessity of creating an addition source of income, the first being agriculture.), SME OneSource incubates small production units as commercial production unit by sourcing minimum number of machines, weighing scale, band sealing machine, bag stitching machine, storage crates and packaging materials with three months of production schedule. Fund for incubation is sourced by SME OneSource through Impact Investors and/or nationalized banks as composite loan for each MPO unit. Minimum investment required to complete three to six months of production to market cycle is Rs. 2.50 lakhs for capital assets and Rs. 2.50 lakhs for direct and indirect expenses.

The above two cases are examples of how successful collaboratives can be established if suitable support is offered. These collaboratives have been successful in creating livelihood. In rural areas, skilling training youth for better opportunities and entrepreneurship, reviving conventional crafts and uplifting the poor through their entrepreneurial skills.

The field survey of these enterprises was done by the authors. It showed that these kinds of ventures have great potential to provide the necessary support, skills and bargaining power to the participants. These benefits are many a time lacking in the case of microlending.

Strengths of Entrepreneurial Models

Going beyond microlending: It has been observed that the microlending is used for consumption and unproductive needs. Microfinance has only partial success in uplifting the poor out of their conditions. Banerjee et al. (2017) stated that the poor do not necessarily have the skills and the drive to become businessmen. Microenterprises are too tiny to provide them capital for reinvestment and growth. Microenterprises cannot stand the competition from the more sophisticated enterprises. The solution to these problems can be collaboratives. Collective ventures can remove the limitations arising at the individual level. In a collaborative enterprise different individuals can use their diverse skills to run a successful enterprise. NGOs behind these collaboratives provide training, for marketing, pricing, reaching for funds, etc. They are also supported by the government under various schemes.

Weaknesses of Entrepreneurial Models

The filed survey revealed that the beneficiaries depended on someone providing them work and income. There were very few women who had the drive to take initiative for going beyond the set pattern of marketing- and revenue-generating models. This was observed even in long-established ventures like Toehold. The organization works for establishing the enterprise and making it participatory but the members rely on somebody leading them and making decisions for them. Their conditions perhaps or their poverty for generations has made them think that someone from outside should help them to improve their situation. The weakness of these ventures is that the members look for an outside leader to guide them and due to this conviction, the success of these ventures is as far as the involvement of the founders in the venture.

Scalability: These kinds of enterprises are at many places in India but they largely remain confined to a certain region, district or village. The same model is not expanded across the country. Hence the scalability remains an issue delimiting its effectiveness to eradicate mass poverty and microlending prevails.

Bank Licensing to MFIs

A recent development in the field of microfinance has been microfinance institutions being converted into small finance banks. In 2014, RBI announced the issue of banking licences to to NBFCs, local area banks and even individuals with experience in banking. Many of the MFIs applied for such licences due to their experience in small ticket lending. The purpose of Small finance banks is to facilitate financial inclusion by providing loans to small business units, small and marginal farmers, micro- and small industries and other unorganized sector entities through high-technology and low-cost operations.

The MFIs were particularly interested in turning to banks because of their ability to raise deposits. This brings down the cost of funds substantially also reduces the dependency on outsourced funds. This is also expected to allow them to lend at lower rates than they do now.

Ideally, as per the RBI norms MFIs are allowed to have interest rate spread of a maximum of 10%. Since the cost of funds to them is approximately 12–14%, most of them can officially charge in the range of 22–24%. If they get a bank licence the cost of funds for them will be less and they will be charging lower lending rates to the micro-finance borrowers. However, in practice the MFI banks face many problems like competition from the banks, low capital adequacy, RBI regulations impinging on the funds and rates, etc.

Bandhan was granted approval in-principle approval by the RBI in April 2014 to set up a bank in the private sector. Bandhan Bank started operations on August 23, 2015. It is possibly the first microlending institution to get a full banking licence in India. As on March 31, 2014, it had a loan book of Rs. 6,200 crore and 5.4 million borrowers. The RBI set the minimum entry capital at Rs. 500 crore. Promoters were required to set up a wholly owned Non-Operative Financial Holding Company (NOFHC). Bandhan Bank was formed under the holding structure of Bandhan Financial Ltd.

Alok Prasad in an interview with The Live Mint (August 24, 2014) stated that the MFIs are eager to have SFB or bank status as the 'non-bank' tag is perceived as negative. The MFIs can shed this perception and build trust with their customers as they will be more closely regulated by the RBI.

The business model of MFIs is tailored to ensure access to financial services, especially credit, needed by vulnerable groups.

According to reports (Unnikrishnan, 2020, Moneycontrol.com dated August 20, 2020), with the RBI lifting restrictions on branch opening, Bandhan Bank is looking to add about 250 outlets in a month. This comes at a time when the microfinance industry is showing signs of stress. Recently Goldman Sachs highlighted key risks to Bandhan Bank including aggressive growth in top-up loans, relapse of slippages in Assam due to floods, social and local issues in home markets, failure to convert depositors into a revenue opportunity over the medium term and lack of synergies in the affordable housing business. In the aftermath of COVID-19, the RBI declared a moratorium on term loan EMIs till August 31, 2020. Banks are suspecting a rise in bad loans once the moratorium is lifted. That's another challenge awaiting Bandhan Bank.

Conclusion

These new developments may result in reducing some portion of financial burden on banks the development of social stock exchange also can be expected to lessen the banks' burden of financing the MFIs and NGOs. They can be free to independently forge into the microlending arena.

Similar can be the case with MFIs converting into banks to bear their own financial burden. Then the MFIs would have alternate sources of funding. However, the role of banks in inclusive finance would not be reduced as they can have direct contact with the poor borrowers instead of indirectly lending them through refinancing. In fact, the development of digital infrastructure would revive the role of banks by removing the erstwhile limitations on their prowess in the financial inclusion.

References

Arner, D. W., Barberis, J., & Buckley, R. P. (2015). The evolution of Fintech: A new post-crisis paradigm. *Georgetown Journal of International Law, 47,* 1271.

Arvidson, M., Lyon, F., McKay, S., & Moro, D. (2013). Valuing the social? The nature and controversies of measuring social return on investment (SROI). *Voluntary Sector Review, 4*(1), 3–18.

Banerjee, A. V., & Duflo, E. (2011). *Poor economics: Rethinking poverty & the ways to end it*. Random House India.

Banerjee, A. V., Breza, E., Duflo, E., & Kinnan, C. (2017). Do credit constraints limit entrepreneurship? Heterogeneity in the returns to microfinance. Heterogeneity in the Returns to Microfinance (September 1, 2017). *Global Poverty Research Lab Working Paper*, 17–104.

Bhatia, V. (Dated 24 February 2020). *Moneycontrol*. India emerges as 3rd largest fintech centre globally. https://www.moneycontrol.com/news/technology/fintech-india-emerges-as-3rd-largest-fintech-centre-globally-4972491.html.

BIS. (2020a). *Payment aspects of financial inclusion in the fintech era*. https://www.bis.org/cpmi/publ/d191.pdf

BIS. (2020b). *How fintech can promote financial inclusion a new report on the opportunities and challenges* (Dated April 15, 2020). https://mondovisione.com/media-and-resources/news/bis-how-fintech-can-promote-financial-inclusion-a-new-report-on-the-opportuni/

Bolton, E., & Savell, L. (2010). *Towards a new social economy. Blended value creation through social impact bonds*. Social Finance Ltd.

Chavan, P., & Ramkumar, R. (2002). Micro-credit and rural poverty: The evidence. *Economic and Political Weekly, 25*, 110–118.

Chiapello, E., & Knoll, L. (2020). Social finance and impact investing. Governing welfare in the era of financialization. *Historical Social Research/Historische Sozialforschung*, *45*(3), 7–30.

Culley. (2011). *Evaluation of the social impact bond: Lessons from planning and early implementation at HMP Peterborough*. RAND Corporation. https://www.rand.org/pubs/research_briefs/RB9637.html.

Deloitte. (2017, July). *Fintech in India, ready for breakout*. https://www2.deloitte.com/in/en/pages/financial-services/articles/fintech-india-ready-for-breakout.html.

Disley, Emma, Rubin, J., Scraggs, E., Burrowes, N., & May Culley, D. (2011). *Evaluation of the social impact bond: Lessons from planning and early implementation at HMP Peterborough*. RAND Corporation.

EducateGirls. (2018). *Report on evaluation of educate girls social impact bond*. https://www.educategirls.ngo/pdf/Educate-Girls-DIB-Final-Evaluation-Report_2018-06-10.pdf.

Financialization of the Public Interest Conference, Hamburg, Germany.

Fraser, A., Tan, S., Lagarde, M., & Mays, N. (2018). Narratives of promise, narratives of caution: A review of the literature on social impact bonds. *Social Policy & Administration, 52*(1), 4–28.

Gustafsson-Wright, E., & Gardiner, S. (2016). *Using impact bonds to achieve early childhood development outcomes in low-and middle-income countries*. Brookings Institution.

Heinrich, C. J., & Choi, Y. (2007). Performance-based contracting in social welfare programs. *The American Review of Public Administration, 37*, 409–435. https://doi.org/10.1177/0275074006297553.

Instiglio. (2015, May). *Educate girls development impact bond improving education for 18,000 children in rajasthan*. https://instiglio.org/educategirlsdib/wp-content/uploads/2016/03/EG-DIB-Design-1.pdf

Karnani, A. (2009). Romanticising the poor harms the poor. *Journal of International Development: The Journal of the Development Studies Association, 21*(1), 76–86.

Khandker, S. R. (1998). Micro-credit programme evaluation: A critical review 1. *IDS Bulletin, 29*(4), 11–20.

Kode, B. (2020). *India fintech forum*. https://indiafintech.com/cth_speaker/bon-credit/.

Lake, R. W. (2016). The subordination of urban policy in the time of financialization. In J. DeFilippis (Ed.), *Urban policy in the time of Obama* (pp. 45–64). University of Minnesota Press.

Lee, C. (2019). Financial inclusion and the rise of independent incomes in rural India through FinTech apps. *The Economic Times*, BFSI.com (Dated November 25, 2019). https://bfsi.economictimes.indiatimes.com/blog/financial-inclusion-and-the-rise-of-independent-incomes-in-rural-india-through-fin-tech-apps/3889.

Lowe, T., Kimmitt, J., Wilson, R., Martin, M., & Gibbon, J. (2018). (in press). The institutional work of creating and implementing social impact bonds. *Policy and Politics*. https://doi.org/10.1332/030557318X15333032765154.

Maier, F., Barbetta, G. P., & Godina, F. (2018). Paradoxes of social impact bonds. *Social Policy & Administration, 52*(7), 1332–1353.

McHugh, N., Sinclair, S., Roy, M., Huckfield, L., & Donaldson, C. (2013). Social impact bonds: A wolf in sheep's clothing? *Journal of Poverty and Social Justice, 21*(3), 247–257. https://doi.org/10.1332/204674313X13812372137921.

McHugh, N., Sinclair, S., Roy, M., Huckfield, L., & Donaldson, C. (2013). Social impact bonds: A wolf in sheep's clothing? *Journal of Poverty and Social Justice, 21*(3), 247–257.

MEDICI Research. (2019, August 20). https://gomedici.com/boosting-financial-inclusion-india-fintech-solution.

Mishra, V. (2019). *Boosting financial inclusion in India: The FinTech Solution.*

Neyland, D. (2017). On the transformation of children at-risk into an investment proposition: A study of social impact bonds as an ante-market device. *Sociological Review, 66*(3), 492–510.

OECD. (2016). *Development aid rises again in 2016 but flows to poorest countries dip.* https://www.oecd.org/dac/development-aid-rises-again-in-2016-but-flows-to-poorest-countries-dip.htm.

Oroxom, R., Glassman, A., & McDonald, L. (2018). *Structuring and funding development impact bonds for health: Nine lessons from Cameroon and beyond.* Center for Global Development.

Pawson, R. (2004). Simple principles for the evaluation of complex programmes. *CIDADES, Comunidades e Territórios*, (8).

Prasad A. (2018). *Interview with the live mint* (Dated August 24, 2014). https://www.thehindubusinessline.com/money-and-banking/50-of-microfinance-institutions-could-convert-to-banks-regulatory-body-ceo/article20850179.ece1. Updated on March 12, 2018, Published on August 24, 2014.

PWC, ASSOCHAM. (May 2019). *Emerging technologies disrupting the financial sector.* https://www.pwc.in/assets/pdfs/consulting/financial-services/fintech/publications/emerging-technologies-disrupting-the-financial-sector.pdf.

Ravi, S., Gustafsson-Wright, E., Sharma, P., & Boggild-Jones, I. (2019). *The Promise of Impact Investing in India*, Brookings India Research Paper No. 072019 (Available at—https://www.brookings.edu/wp-content/uploads/2019/07/The-promise-of-impact-investing-in-India.pdf).

Saal, Matthew et al. (2017, August). Digital financial services: Challenges and opportunities for emerging markets banks. *EM Compass Note No. 42, International Finance Corporation.*

Sanderson, I. (2000). Evaluation in complex policy systems. *Evaluation, 6*(4), 433–454.

SEBI. (2020, June). *Report of the working group on social stock exchange.* Ishaat Hussain. https://www.sebi.gov.in/reports-and-statistics/reports/jun-2020/report-of-the-working-group-on-social-stock-exchange_46751.html.

Sharma T. (2020). *Explained: What are social stock exchanges and how do they work*. https://www.moneycontrol.com/news/business/markets/explained-what-are-social-stock-exchanges-and-how-they-work-5507931.html.

Shortall, S., & Warner, M. E. (2010). Social inclusion or market competitiveness? A comparison of rural development policies in the European Union and the United States. *Social Policy & Administration, 44*, 575–597. https://doi.org/10.1111/PublicAdministration,37,409-435. doi:10.1177/0275074006297553.

Tan, S., Fraser, A., McHugh, N., & Warner, M. (2019). Widening perspectives on social impact bonds. *Journal of Economic Policy Reform*. https://doi.org/10.1080/17487870.2019.1568249.

Tse, A. E., & Warner, M. E. (2018). The razor's edge: Social impact bonds and the financialization of early childhood services. *Journal of Urban Affairs, 1–17*. https://doi.org/10.1080/07352166.2018.1465347.

Unnikrishnan, D. (Updated August 20, 2020). *Bandhan Bank 5 years on: The story of a sweet shop owner's son who built a thriving private lender Moneycontol.com*. https://www.moneycontrol.com/news/business/bandhan-bank-5-years-on-the-story-of-a-sweet-shop-owners-son-who-built-a-thriving-private-lender-5733211.html.

Warner, M. E. (2013). Private finance for public goods: Social impact bonds. *Journal of Economic Policy Reform, 16*(4), 303–319.

CHAPTER 8

Reimagining the Banking Business Model

The Context: Existential Crisis for the Microfinance Sector

The question of the future of sustaining microfinance activities in India has been at the forefront, particularly since the COVID-19 pandemic. The entire inclusive finance ecosystem has been facing existential problems during the crisis.

A large part of the microcredit (75%) is used for consumption purposes and repayments usually depend on the monthly wages received by the borrowers. Through backward and forward linkages among the sectors, wage earners in both formal and informal sectors are dependent on the financial health of the corporate sector. Any problem with the corporate finances, in turn, is reflected in the quality of banking sector's assets. Thus, the balance sheets of the MFI sector are eventually linked with the balance sheets of the banking sector. During the lockdown, repayments either stopped or reduced in many cases and the cycle of earning and lending of MFIs was disrupted.

This time the crisis is at a mega level as compared with the Andhra crisis. Due to contagion of the finances of MFIs, NBFCs and the banking sector, the defaults are making an impact on the entire system. The latter involves not only the microlending institutions but also countless individuals. The sheer magnitude of this crisis calls for an urgent reconsideration of the strategies of institutions in the inclusive finance arena. The

L. Kulkarni and V. C. Joshi, *Inclusive Banking In India*,
https://doi.org/10.1007/978-981-33-6797-5_8

government and banks did step into assist the institutions but in the long run banks, being the direct or indirect financiers of the entire inclusive finance system, need to adopt a far-reaching strategy. The current chapter proposes that a somewhat bold and unconventional approach needs to be adopted by banks if the system is to come out of this turmoil unscathed. We propose a bank business model that moots a transformation in the perception, motivation, thought process and behaviour of the banks.

The chapter discusses the concept and importance of the bank business models, analyses commercial banks' existing business model in India, refers to the factors challenging the profitability and solvency of banks and proposes a transformation of the existing business model. The current section discusses what a bank business model is and why a bank must develop a structured business model.

Business Model of a Bank

A bank business model is a blue print of how a bank sees its client base, serves it by designing its products, delivers those products and creates value for itself as well as the customer.

The business model of a firm specifies its customer base, provides clarity regarding the value created by it for the customer and how it can create that value at a cost justifiable to the customer (Drucker, 2017).

Bank business models are not static but stable over time under the influence of a complex mix of both exogenous and endogenous pressures. They have to respond to sector specific factors like competition, changing objectives, work culture, technological change and banking sector regulation. A business model must respond to macroeconomic factors like financial sector reforms, global business cycles, macroeconomic policy, etc. (Thygesen et al., 2013).

In bank-led economies like the Indian economy, a systematic analysis of bank business models is required for at least three reasons, i.e.

1. The effect of a business strategy of a bank is not limited just to its own profits but has a much wider effect on the economy. The banking sector is interlinked with the household as well as the corporate sectors through the flow of credit and deposits. In spite of the growth of non-bank institutions and capital market, this sector has a major share in credit and savings in India. Even during the pandemic, according to the latest reports (*The Times of India*, dated

3rd August 2020) in the financial year 2020,[1] household savings were composed of 52.6% deposits with banks, 23.2% in life insurance, 13.4% in the form of currency and 7% in mutual funds. Given the slowdown in insurance and mutual fund savings, there is a strong likelihood that the share of bank deposits in household savings could rise. The share of individuals in total bank credit increased to 40.1% in March 2020 from 37.4% a year ago and 30.8% five years back. Thus, the macroeconomic implications of banking business make it essential to analyse its business model for the regulators and monetary policy formulation.

2. Irrespective of the significance of the banking sector in the Indian economy, a methodical discussion on the bank business model for Indian banks is hardly found in the literature. In fact, usually for a common man it is difficult to perceive a bank as a commercial firm. Developing a business model for the banking sector is perhaps overlooked on account of its tight regulation.
3. Studies pertaining to the banking sector in the western countries like the European Union and USA discuss various bank business models that exist there. Studies published after the financial crisis in 2008 discussed how the bank business models have been changing from fund-based interest income to non-interest income (Ayadi & De Groen, 2014; Gamra & Plihon, 2011). They show the banking sector and business models in western countries where the former is dominated by the private sector banks. However, studies on bank business models in developed economies are hardly relevant for application to the banking sector in India. Hence, it is necessary to discuss the bank business model in the context of inclusive finance by the scheduled commercial banks.

Current Issues Impinging on Inclusive Banking in India and Need for a New Business Model

The importance of inclusive finance for economic development is well accepted. There are policy measures from the government as well as NGOs and NBFC sector but the efforts have been misguided. The

[1] https://timesofindia.indiatimes.com/business/india-business/at-rs-6l-cr-banks-fresh-fds-in-q1-double-from-last-year Updated: Aug 3, 2020, 12:46 IST.

following discussion addresses some important issues related to inclusive banking:

1. Banks as lenders to the entire inclusive finance sector:

   The penetration of banks and microfinance in India has been increasing at an exponential rate. However, the data shows that informal credit has not budged. There is an elastic demand for credit from the base of the pyramid population. If we look at the data for the last few decades, we see that the number of institutions lending to the poor has been increasing, in case of SHGs and microfinance institutions (NBFC, MFIs and NGOs-MFIs).

   The sector as an industry providing credit to the poor is thriving. However, the non-bank microlending institutions depend on banks for financing. Hence, ultimately banks lend to the poor either directly through priority sector lending schemes or indirectly through the microlending institutions (Fig. 8.1). The role of commercial banks in financial inclusion is thus largely underestimated.

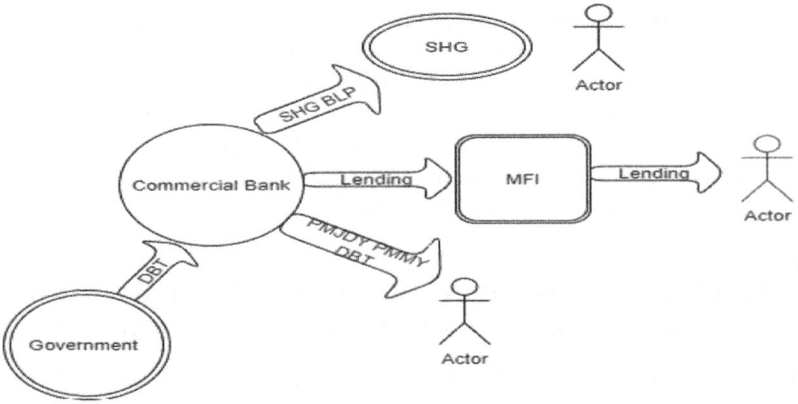

Fig. 8.1 Inclusive finance by banks' direct/indirect funding (*Source* Indicative illustration by authors)

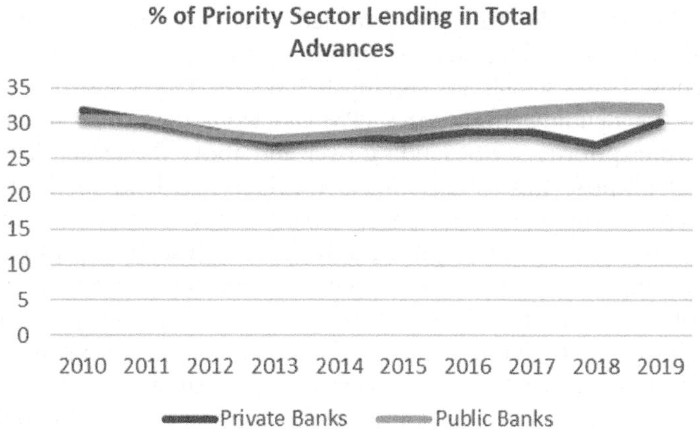

Fig. 8.2 Stagnant priority sector lending (*Source* Based on statistical tables related to Banks in India, RBI Database)

2. Priority Sector Lending—A misguiding indicator

> Loans and advances are the primary source of revenue for a bank. Credit by banks is also important for economic growth as it fuels production and employment. Priority sector lending shows little difference between public and private sector banks. One cannot arrive at any clear conclusion about contribution of the public as well as private banks' lending to the vulnerable sector (Fig. 8.2).

Priority sector lending data is misleading for at least two reasons. Firstly, the current definition of priority sector includes a wide range of enterprises. According to the RBI circular (dated 7 July 2016) lending to transport operators and other allied industries to agriculture also falls under it.[2] This has induced banks—public and private alike—to lend large amounts to transport finance companies and even MSEB under the priority sector heading. The interest rates are not subsidized anymore for this lending. Thus, the data reported on priority sector lending hardly reflects any special treatment to the underprivileged borrowers or weaker sections.

[2] RBI, Master Direction FIDD.CO.Plan.1/04.09/01/2016-17 dated July 7, 2016 (updated as on December 04, 2018).

Secondly, the RBI has provided a mechanism to the banks to cover the shortfall in lending target for their priority sector lending. Those banks which are lagging behind the target can buy Priority Sector Lending Certificates (PSLCs) from the banks which have surplus priority sector lending over and above the target. The original purpose was to incentivize the banks to lend to the priority sector. Thus, even if on paper a bank has met the target, in practice it might have bought the PSLCs only. Just the report of banks meeting the priority sector target does not imply that they are truly committed to the financial inclusion objective. Intricacies of the priority sector lending data indicate that these norms are not as effective as expected in achieving inclusive banking.

3. Dwindling interest rates and Low Net interest margin: Interest rates are continuously falling due to adverse shocks to the economy. During the pandemic with the global slowdown, interest rates in India also have a downward pressure to promote economic revival. This creates a pressure on net interest margin and profitability of the banks from the conventional business (Fig. 8.3).

In a recessionary environment, the central bank reduces repo rate, i.e., the rate at which it lends to banks. In 2019, RBI reduced it thrice to reach 4%, which is the lowest since 2010. When the RBI reduces the repo rate, banks can borrow from it at a cheaper

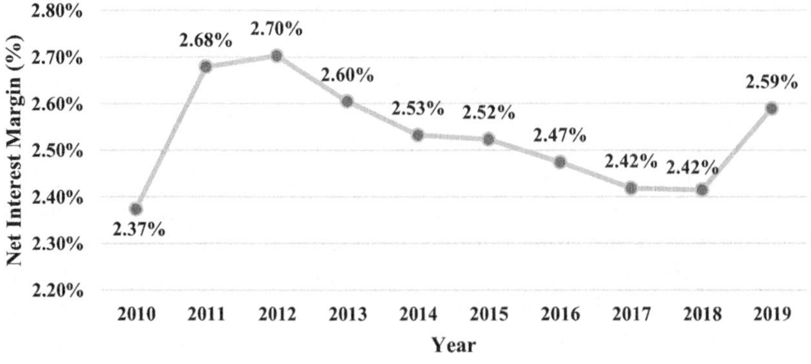

Fig. 8.3 Net Interest Margin, 2010 to 2019 (*Source Reports of trends and progress of banking in India, 2009–2010 to 2018–2019.* Reserve Bank of India, www.rbi.org.in)

rate. Such a reduction in repo rate signalizes the banks to reduce the lending rate which is expected to encourage investment and economic growth. The net interest margin is the difference between the interest earned on loans and interest paid on the deposits by banks. Since 2011 up to 2018 the net interest margin declined. This means that banks are getting less revenue from their core activity of lending and deposit mobilization. Hence, they have to start looking at other avenues for earnings such as fees and commissions. They can also explore newer business strategies to expand business.

4. Revenue Diversification: Rising risk due to dependence on pro-cyclical source of income

Due to low net interest margins, banks are increasing their fee and commission income.

Fig. 8.4 shows that 11% of private sector revenue comes from the fees and commission income. In public sector banks it is approximately 5%, while 12% of the total income accrues from the non-fund sources other than interest income. Banks increasingly rely on the non-interest/fee-based income for their revenue.

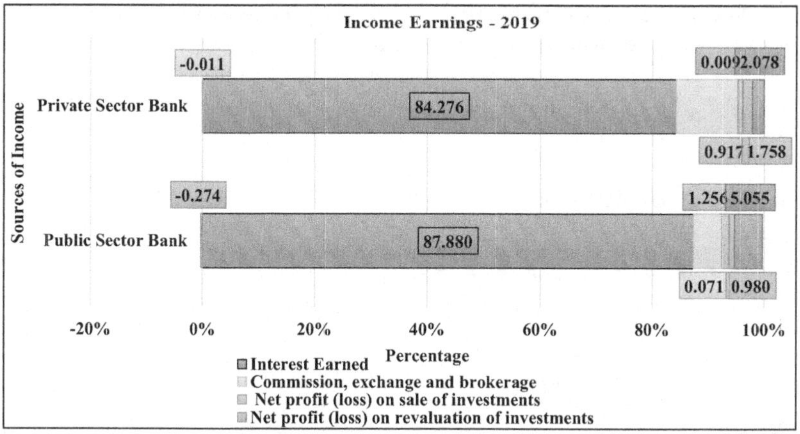

Fig. 8.4 Revenue Mix of Commercial Banks—2019 (*Source* Based on *Earnings and expenses of scheduled commercial banks, 2019*, Reserve Bank of India. Retrieved from: www.rbi.org.in)

To adjust for the increasing competition and lowering net interest margins, banks rely on unconventional non-bank avenues like insurance, investment banking, asset management, etc. The diversion of bank revenue away from the fund-based activities to fee-based activities is a matter of concern as it proves to be pro-cyclical and increases revenue fluctuations making banks vulnerable to business cycles.

5. High provision coverage ratio encroaching the operating profit of public sector banks

Operating profits of banks are the difference between their revenues and operating costs. They are a measure of efficiency.

Operating profit = (Interest earned + Other income)−(Interest paid)−Operating expenses.

In the case of banks' profit and loss accounts, the provision for NPAs reduces the profits to that extent.

Operating profit−Provisions & contingencies = Bank profit

Fig. 8.5 shows that the provision coverage ratio is higher for the public sector banks than the private sector banks, and it continues to increase. Provisions are a portion of their operating profits set aside as a provision against bad loans. Thus, in the bank balance sheets the NPAs are reduced to that extent.

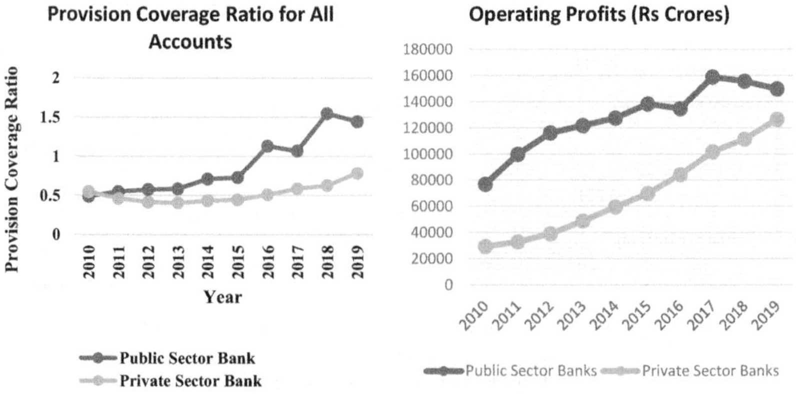

Fig. 8.5 Provision of coverage ratio and operating profits: public vs. private sector banks (*Source* Calculated from *Earnings and expenses of scheduled commercial banks, 2019*. Reserve Bank of India www.rbi.org.in)

The provisional coverage ratio (PCR) of scheduled commercial banks increased drastically from 48.3% in March 2018 to 60.6% in March 2019 (RBI, Financial Stability Report, June 2019), increasing the resilience of the banking sector.

Though it is a risk management measure, it impinges on the operating profit. As can be observed from Figure 8.5, the operating profit of the public sector banks is higher than the private sector banks but the profit after provisioning is negative. Thus, even though the operating profit of the public sector banks is high, provisions due to high NPAs eat into their profits.

6. Competition from entry of non-bank payment platforms and alternate lending channels

   Although the share of banking sector in India is more than 50% in credit and deposits, the Fintech revolution is slowly but steadily snatching away the business of payments and transactions. Non-bank payment platforms, like Paytm, Google Pay, PayPal, etc., are popular. In the business of lending, also P2P transactions are gaining a foothold. These developments provide a wider choice of financial services, and lending and borrowing options to the customer.

In Search of a New Model

The above discussion highlights that:

1. Banks in India have never independently thought about devising a business model. They have been managing somehow by following the RBI and government directives and facing the winds of change passively.
2. The new world of low interest rates, high volatility and cut throat competition makes it indispensable for banks to change their passive stance and actively think about how they will foster their business in the coming years.
3. The pandemic shock has created uncertainty all over the system, aggravating the already existing problems of commercial banks.

This entails searching for a new paradigm.

New Approach, New Narrative

The phrase 'bottom of the pyramid' or 'Base of the pyramid' (BoP) was popularized by C. K. Prahalad and Hart (2002) in his seminal work *The Fortune at the Bottom of the Pyramid—Eradicating poverty through profits*. The concept implied at least two significant ideas. Firstly, businesses can find a sizable opportunity at the bottom of the pyramid which is essentially the low-income segment of the population. Secondly, when the businesses approach the bottom population in search of profitable opportunity, it benefits the low-income customers as their needs are served.

Along these lines in the banking sector by recognizing the base of the pyramid as a potential emerging market, banks can increase their market share or enter new markets, reaping benefits for themselves as well as for the poor.

Thus far, the bottom of the pyramid customer is never considered to be a viable market for the banking business. Banks neglected its significance as a business segment though had to cater to this customer as a mandatory requirement imposed by the government initiatives for financial inclusion.

The New Narrative

We propose to bring about a change in the above narrative. We propose changing the jargon or the nomenclature, calling this segment the 'Bulk' of the pyramid instead of its 'Base' or 'Bottom'. The latter terms attach hierarchy to our understanding and connote something that is located at the end, the lowest part, to be approached only after the top part. The bulk in our inverted pyramid structure does away with the hierarchy in the structure as also discards the judgement in the meaning. Henceforth, in this book the BoP is not the 'Base' of the pyramid but the 'Bulk' of the population. It indicates a market segment that is a large portion. As the first step to the new business model, we propose that the perspective of banks must change accordingly (Fig. 8.6).

'Bulk of the population' segment is relevant for the model. Thus, the other layers are shown as broad classes without specifying the customers. Banks should consider the bulk of the population (BoP) customers as their core client base and directly target them for the future business. Therefore, this segment is unbanked and can be considered a possible 'blue ocean'.

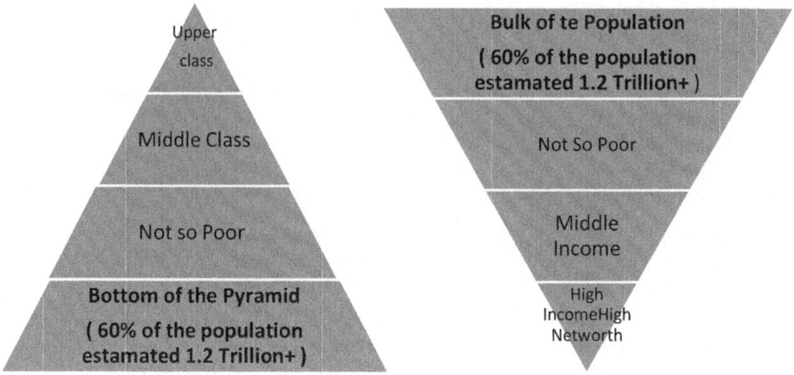

Fig. 8.6 Changing the narrative (*Source* Adapted from Prahalad, 2005)

Bulk of the Population—A Blue Ocean in Banking

The blue ocean strategy, developed by Mauborgne and Kim (2005), advises organizations on how to tackle competition. According to this management strategy, red ocean is the existing saturated market space while blue oceans are unexplored market segments that have opportunity and growth. In the banking sector, the red ocean is the business segment consisting of the regular customers, competition and macro-environment that leave little scope for growth. The blue ocean represents the market segment that is an untapped market space and has potential for demand creation and profitable growth. For banks in India even though the bulk of the pyramid segment is not new, it has never been looked upon as a profitable business prospect. Even though the bulk of the pyramid customers already exist in government schemes like PMJDY, the perspective of banks to look at this market segment should be changed, and they must realize that this segment is the blue ocean of the banking sector that has so far remained untapped.

We suggest that banks can consider the bulk of the pyramid customers their blue ocean as this segment is still unexplored from a business viewpoint. There is enough potential for its growth over a period of time. The strategy should be to create high value but charge low to the customers (Fig. 8.7).

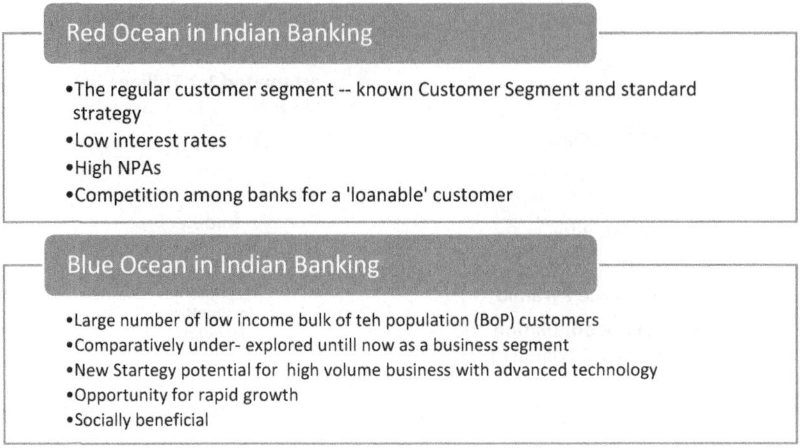

Fig. 8.7 Comparing blue oceans with red oceans (*Source* Compiled by the authors based on www.blueoceanstrategy.com)

Development of a Business Model

A generic business model visualizes two sets of factors. One set consists of those components generating utility for a business, viz. customer, value proposition and channel. The second set generates costs, viz. procuring key resources, roping in key partnerships and executing key activities. Price will be determined at a balance of these two sets to generate value to both business as well as its customer. Success in arriving at this price will determine the success and sustainability of the business model.

Business Model for Inclusive Banking in India

To quote Raghuram Rajan, 'Expanding access to finance to small and medium enterprises, the unorganized sector, the poor, and remote and underserved areas of the country through technology, new business practices, and new organizational structures; that is, financial inclusion is the fifth pillar of RBI's financial policy' (Rajan, 2017, p. 15).

To make the model easier to understand, we visualize a hypothetical bank in India called ANY BANK. We assume that this bank is facing a challenging situation as described in Sects. 8.1 and 8.2. To face it ANY BANK transforms its conventional outlook and decides to adopt a new business model. It realizes that the bulk of the population (BoP) is the blue ocean for business and plans a strategy to launch a new scheme for it. (We call this *New Scheme*). The bank dedicates an entire section, department or wing (here named as Sabka Sath) for this 'business'. The already existing PMJDY would provide the Bank the minimum required information and also some of the benefits to which the account holders are entitled. Its new scheme will be built on this information, collect the required particulars and ensure that the eligibility norms are met.

New Scheme is a basic account like the earlier PMJDY but has the full functionality necessary for core banking. Banks already have a product in the form of PMJDY designed to serve this segment and are indirectly operating in the inclusive finance segment. They are already implementing the PMJDY, financing NGOs, MFIs and SHGs, and lending to the MSMEs under the priority sector lending norms. But all this is done as a mandatory requirement and not willingly. To show the targeted achievements under the priority sector, this Bank lends to the transport finance companies and larger industries. The PMJDY accounts are opened but no one bothers about the transactions and inactive accounts. The borrowers who do enter the bank office are discouraged by the apathy of the staff. The new business model proposes a fresh outlook.

PMJDY accounts can be made functional if the banks change their perception, stop considering it an obligation and start treating the 'Bulk of the population' (BoP) customers at par with the regular customer. The value additions are for the convenience of customers who always want to check the balances. They can do so at the access points or with their mobile sets. Facilities under the PMJDY would continue under the new scheme, and in addition, banks would provide lending and other benefits. Thus, PMJDY would provide the bank with the minimum required information about the BoP segment and also some of the benefits to which the account holder is entitled.

The Banks' new scheme will be built on this information, collect the required particulars and ensure that the eligibility norms are met.

Thus, the Sabka Sath wing will offer accessible accounts with minimum eligibility criteria, offering online and offline withdrawals, competitive interest rates and self-respect to the customers (Fig. 8.8).

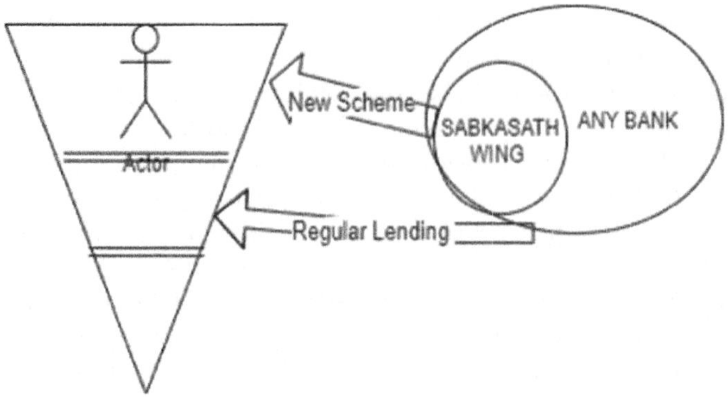

Fig. 8.8 Serving the bulk of the population (*Source* The authors)

Can the Bulk of the Population (BoP) Be the Blue Ocean of the Banking Industry?

If this bank looks beyond the set pattern of thinking, it will be able to consider the BoP customer segment as the blue ocean. In fact, the latter can be developed as a blue ocean by any type of bank—public sector bank, private sector bank or even a foreign bank. We build up a step-by-step business model for this Bank.

ANY BANK will establish a new wing specially for this blue ocean business. We have conjured a name for this special segment 'Sabka Sath'. The business model for it is proposed below. Sabka Sath is not a microfinance institution but a special wing of a commercial bank. This is a new approach since in the past banks maintained their misconception that microfinance activities could not be undertaken by them because a labour intensive work system made the operation uneconomical. They were also complacent because by outsourcing the operations to microfinance firms and financing MFIs, the main objective of microlending was achieved.

Today this situation has transformed due to the advent of mobile banking and technology. Public sector bank staff costs are already reduced by approximately 16% and even less at 11% for the private sector banks from the earlier range of 60–70%. This makes it possible for banks to adopt microlending operations directly rather than indirectly through the MFIs.

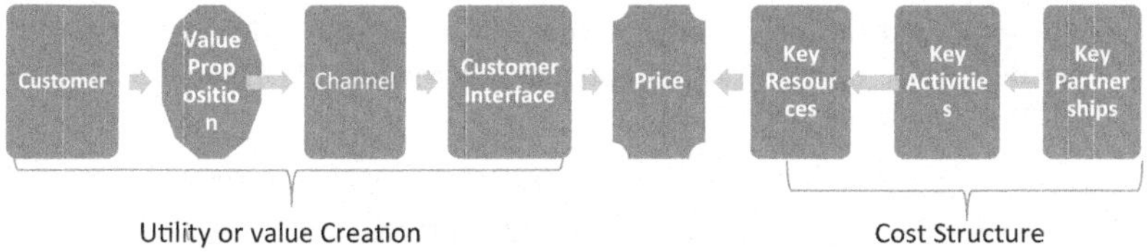

Fig. 8.9 Components of business model (*Source* Illustration by the authors based on Osterwalder & Pigneur, 2010)

The following diagram summarizes the business model canvas—a popular tool developed by Osterwalder and Pigneur (2010) (Fig. 8.9).

Obviously, in businesses like banking, the business canvas has to be carefully developed as the products (loans and advances) are intertemporal and generate risk. Its adaptation will be insightful yet complicated in the case of inclusive banking. The next section attempts at building such a business model canvas visualizing the Bulk of the pyramid bank customers as the core clientele for the commercial banks.

The following discussion suggests a step-by-step model for the hypothetical Sabka Sath wing of the ANY BANK for business development in bulk of the population segment.

Identifying and Nurturing the Blue Ocean and Specifying the Customer

The Sabka Sath wing will focus on the thus far unbanked and underprivileged population in India as its blue ocean customer segment. Although this segment is not a newly found blue ocean, we can treat it so because banks have never explored it from a business perspective. This may not be the universal population at the bottom of the pyramid.

In 1998 Prahalad defined the base of the pyramid in terms of those whose spending on daily consumption is less than $2.

> The Bank looks at the New Scheme as a retail banking product aimed at low-income earners. It is designed to provide an affordable transactional product to all income brackets. They might be migrants, seasonal informal sector workers and underemployed or seasonally employed. According to the World Bank estimates, more than 60% of the population or 750 million people earned Rs. 45.5 or less per day in 2011. In the context

of the proposed business model, verification of papers and corroboration is needed while opening an account and borrowing. Data collected for PMJDY accounts can be utilized.

Value Proposition

Banks must be sensitive to the needs of the BoP customers and engage closely with the lives of their customers (Prahalad, 2005).

In India we already have the product in the form of zero balance PMJDY accounts. Banks should try to examine why their usage is low and try to provide services accordingly. A bank can self-assess in terms of its delivery of the PMJDY and also its experience of PMJDY as a product.

Referring to Prahalad's 4 As, the product must have,

a. Acceptability: It should be useful and designed to cater to the specific needs of the customers.
b. Availability: It should be easily accessible at minimal costs and effort.
c. Awareness: Customers should understand the product clearly.
d. Affordability: Customers should find the product worth its value for their paying capacities.

To make the business model viable, a bank has to ensure that the product or service is tailored to the needs of the BoP. It is also called the window of opportunity for the BoP. This implies that banks would be able to cultivate the BoP market if the customers find the product useful. The window of opportunity for the customer will create utility of the product or service for him. Utility of the business depends on three factors, viz. value proposition, channels and customer interface (Themaat et al., 2013). Founders of most MFIs know the pulse of their BoP clients. Bankers have no choice but to leave the offices and engage with the people. Interaction with gram sevaks, panchayat officials or district level officials functioning at the village level will be useful.

The Product—What Do Bulk of the Customers Want?

Our hypothetical bank gains insight into the lives of the BoP customers and understands what they want and why they don't use certain products like PMJDY, while still saving and borrowing from MFIs and moneylenders. It makes a self-assessment based on gaps in the existing banking services to cater to the requirements of the BoP. It is evident from surveys and studies that customers want a product that is simple, accessible, friendly, and expect the service personnel to treat them with dignity and operate at convenient timings in a familiar language.

Sabka Sath Bank has to simplify the product. The PMJDY will assist banks to provide the required particulars which will have to be supplemented by banks. Taking into account the customer perceptions, it will launch the novel idea of access points. This is the first step to make the value proposition acceptable to the BoP customers.

The customer will go to the access point in his/her local area, submit the Aadhaar and register with the biometric. Thus, opening a new account should take less than 15 minutes and should be completely a paperless process. The agent at the access point will be entering all the information into the system. This is a process designed to make the customer feel welcome and safe.

The process of opening a New Scheme will be simple and involve minimal paperwork. The accounts can be opened in bank branches and places of frequent visits like the local market. Agents to serve at the access points will be recruited from within the community. At the access points other services offered by the banks will be known to the borrowers, and they should be guided to avail of them with the help of their mobile sets (e.g. Kenya, MPesa). Sales agents will take pictures of customers' identity documents which will then be electronically stored, thereby eliminating expensive paperwork and document filing. The agents will also record their biometric impressions and UID numbers. They will be electronically stored on the bank server and accounts will be opened. The customer will be provided with a card. She can transact business using this card along with the biometric. Misuse/frauds will be curtailed because of electronic records, biometric identification and UID. In India we are already using this kind of infrastructure for the registration of property. The facility for registration is available in small shops with a government license from where the papers, biometric, etc., are forwarded online to the concerned department after which the property registration is completed. Accessibility of the access point is expected to encourage the people to use their accounts.

The New Scheme will be accessible at the access points established by the bank in convenient places frequented by the targeted customers, e.g. petty shops, bakeries and flour mills in urban and rural slums, *vastis* and *mohallas*. Access points will be established in addition to the existing points such as automatic teller machines (ATMs) and branches.

As the first point of contact with the bank, access point would work as an annex to the branch and work initially in proximity to an existing branch. Thus, it will not replace a branch. It will be a low cost mobile centre manned with a local community agent who will help the customers in opening the account and verify the completion of documents, train the customers in using the online/mobile banking and inform them about the various schemes of the bank. It will be the duty of the local agents (details given further) to explain to the borrowers what their responsibilities will be.

Channel: Awareness and Availability

The core requirements of the channel component are awareness and availability through distribution, marketing and awareness activities. Here, traditional marketing through radio/television set and local agents will work. The 'Lays' model of making the product accessible and visible will work for Sabka Sath. In countries like India peer feedback and mouth-to-mouth publicity for the account and the bank will be the most effective channel. SHGs and MFIs have thrived relying on them.

Customer Interface

Customer interface in these services must be friendly to the semi-literate local language customers. It should empower them in negotiation and give them the control to make informed decisions.

The Sabka Sath Bank customers' interface will be paperless. Agents at the access points will assist them to fill the forms and open the accounts. Use of biometric controls such as fingerprint technology and cameras will ensure security. Agents and access points will be accessible. There will not be office timings or holidays, allowing customers flexibility and control to do banking when they wish to. In this model tellers are practically the access point operators. They are to be selected from the local community so that they have a good understanding of the customers. For borrowings, the customers can enter their biometric and the amount of loan required. The bank will process the credit history of the customer with its data. All this can be processed in a day with technology and the amount will be credited for the customer. All the transactions will be cashless to avoid frauds. Credit will be made to any of the UPI platforms so that the customers can transact money.

Pricing Strategy: Pricing the Bank's Products Is the Key Puzzle to Be Solved

The price has to be profitable for the bank on the one hand, and acceptable and affordable to the customer on the other. To achieve this, the bank should examine the MFIs' pricing strategy. So far it has been presumed that banks would have to charge low interest rates for the BoP customers. However, MFIs have burst this myth. They charge interest rates in the range of 14–26%. Evidently, they are not only viable but also profitable. After 2014 RBI has regulated the lending rates charged by them.

The regulation gives two alternative mechanisms to MFIs to arrive at the rate. They are required to either charge a maximum of 10% margin over and above their cost of funds, or they have to accept the rate calculated by multiplying the average base rate of the five largest commercial banks (by assets) with a constant factor 2.75. The average base rate of the five largest banks is declared quarterly by the RBI based on the last working day of the previous quarter to decide the interest rate for the current quarter.

To retain a reasonable profit margin, costs have to be kept minimum. In fact, this is true for any business. In the case of the BoP segment, the costs of monitoring, underwriting, collecting credit history, etc., are high. The MFIs could manage it successfully because of their relationship lending and the proximity of their officials to the borrowing groups. Banks being formal institutions rely on transactional rather than relationship lending, and thus a thin filed customer becomes a loss-making proposition for them.

In our model, the Sabka Sath wing will charge lending interest rates and transaction fees that will be significantly lower than those of its competitors. It will not charge fees for the New Scheme access card purchases and cash withdrawals. It will offer positive savings deposit rate to encourage savings.

Even though the amounts are small, lending spreads over a period of time. Therefore, banks should ensure that the low cost long term funding is availed of through the channels of long term funding. The asset liability mismatch in short run deposits and long run loans is always a matter of concern for the bankers. This mismatch is reflected in portfolios of the microlending segment as well. Eventually for a long term need due to asset liability mismatch, the possibility of raising funds from the social equity market can be explored as discussed in Chapter 7 of this book.

The model conceives the following HR and administrative infrastructure for the Sabka Sath wing of the ANY BANK to deliver to the BoP customer.

Administrative Infrastructure for BoP Segment

Based on the experience of the successful inclusive banking models in some countries, we can develop a model administrative infrastructure (Fredericks, 2015). Initially there will be a core team of permanent employees assisted by a second team of sales agents. Various alternative frameworks can then be evolved. The idea is to replace high cost bank infrastructure by outsourcing the operations and using technology to reduce costs. This structure can be replicated around the country in each district of each state. The following structure is visualized for initial stages where mobile banking is hampered. However, the model visualizes reliance on technology rather than brick and mortar structures.

The core team can consist of a manager in charge of the inclusive banking sales strategy for the area falling under his or her responsibility, and locally recruited employees known as business development officers. Community agents will also be the first line of contact with the access point owners in their area.

While the agents will move around, the access points will be stationary points in the areas most frequented by the borrowers. The agents should be young and may be formerly unemployed or partially employed. They must be trained to respect the customer, educate her about the opening of the account and the use of the electronic kiosk to withdraw money and apply for loans. Once briefed, the customers will be able to operate at their own with assistance from the community agent.

As community agents will be local youths, so they will interact freely in the customers' language and establish a rapport with them. Their primary function will be to sign up potential customers to the *New Scheme* and assist account holders with information when needed. Community agent teams are to be equipped with branded sheds or stalls, giving them a visible presence in public places like market yards, APC markets in rural areas, small grocery stores, etc. In this way, the Sabka Sath wing will try to overcome the main obstacle for banks in being closely associated with the community. Prudent use of technology and administrative infrastructure can bring the costs down.

Infrastructure is important for achieving minimum cost without compromising quality. With the use of technology, mobile operations will be the mainstay for reduction in costs, and the requisite infrastructure will evolve and staff skilled over a period of time.

Use of Technology to Reduce Costs

The bank will operate Sabka Sath wing on the basis of advanced technology and will not need bricks and mortar infrastructure to do its business. It can operate with minimum offices and branches. The head office will only be at a zonal level. The state and district level offices will coordinate the transactions in their areas with the help of technological platforms.

To make the proposed model a reality, a precondition is that banks should collaborate with Fintech firms. The financial technology would be used for a centralized system of data and book clearance, and customers can not only deposit their money anywhere through the local access points, but also get loans sanctioned and credited to their accounts anywhere. The ANY BANK will not need to keep cash on the premises which will allow it to reduce costs by having less security. The model visualizes minimum costs of a branch as cash is not deposited there. Instead, cash deposits will be directly deposited in a safety vault and withdrawable only from the ATMs or retailers.

Key Resources Component

A highly motivated and well trained staff will be kept. The entire system will depend on motivating, training and developing an ethical work culture. The focus should not be mainly on formal higher education degrees but on understanding of the local customer and the willingness to work for him.

The key activities component describes all the activities that organization will have to complete to ensure that the business model operates effectively. Sabka Bank will develop a centralized computer system that facilitates paperless transactions.

Key Partners

Key Partners are the network of partners and suppliers which the organization needs to make sure that its business model works effectively. In India wherever possible banks can use existing infrastructure—BCs and young members from SHGs linked to banks. Sabka Sath can increase its reach by collaborating with retailers and by using their infrastructure. It can extend its network to places where its customers can withdraw money without large infrastructural investments.

Sabka Sath will keep the withdrawal charges near zero for cash withdrawals from secure access points. It may adopt the model of partnership with established card companies like Master Card to develop customized cards to cater to the population in remote areas.

The above discussion is based on a business model canvas and has focussed on the staff, administrative set up, infrastructure, etc. An important part of this model building exercise is the consideration of financial feasibility.

Financial Model

A general view of bank's profit and loss: A simplified version of a bank's profit and loss account is shown below. This simplified version deals with broad categories of income and expenditure heads in the income statement of a typical bank.

Profit/Loss of a bank = (Interest earned + Other Income)−(Interest Expended + Operating Expenses)

For example, in 2019 taking all PSBs together, we have

(Interest earned + Other income)−Interest expended−Operating cost = Operating profit = (681778.97 + 94024.85)−450613.59−175386.44 = 149803.80

Interest earned is a function of the rate of interest and volume of advances.

Interest paid is the function of the rate of interest on deposits, average amount of deposit and number of deposits.

Potential Financial Viability

Thus far banks have generally believed that the microlending business is not profitable. However, it can turn into a profitable business strategy.

The lending to the poor by formal institutions fails because of moral hazard and incorrect selection. The poor by definition do not have assets to pledge as collateral and so the banks rely on their screening and monitoring. Since the costs are high, the resulting interest rates are not affordable for the poor borrowers and banks do not lend them.

Thus, the two constraints of formal lending are:

1. Low-income borrowers do not have assets for collateral.
2. Their screening and monitoring costs are exorbitant.

We compare the microlending–microdeposits business model of banks with the business model of the MFIs to get an idea of financial viability of the Sabka Sath wing.

Comparison with the MFI Business

1. Net interest income depends on the interest earned and interest paid. In the case of the Sabka Sath transactions, the lending rates would be competitive with the NBFC lenders in both the formal and informal sectors. RBI sets the average base rate for the NBFCs-MFIs on the basis of the average of base rate of the five largest commercial banks. For instance, the average base rate of 8.76% was declared by the Reserve Bank of India on March 31st for NBFCs-MFIs to be charged from their borrowers for the quarter beginning April 1, 2020.

   The NBFC MFIs are allowed to charge up to 10% margin on this rate. According to the MFIN Report Q4 (2020), the rates are around 24–25%. But the cost of capital is around 14–15%. The Sabka Sath lending rate can be far lower than these rates and still be profitable because the cost of funds is less for the bank than for MFIs (The calculation of interest by most MFIs does not consider

Table 8.1 Simple model of Sabka Sath financial viability

	NBFC MFI (based on MFIN Micrometer, March 2020) (%)	*Sabka Sath Model*
Cost of funds	14–15	6% rate of interest paid on BoP deposits
Lending rate	24–25	12–15% rate of interest received on BoP loans

Source Indicative illustration by the authors

reducing balance and hence the effective lending rate is very high for the end borrower).

We postulate that Sabka Sath pays 6% on the savings deposits of BoP customers and charges approximately 14–15% on the loans taken by the BoP customers (Table 8.1). The operating costs of the Sabka Sath wing will be less than the conventional bank or MFI. Hence, the profit margin will be financially viable.

Comparison with the Conventional Bank Business

- Operating costs of existing PSBs are approximately 16% on staff and 11% on administration. These costs are assumed to be almost half for the Sabka Sath wing of the bank due to branchless banking and local access points.
- The cost of processing loans will not affect the overall profit as the loan amounts are small. These costs can be ignored as lending will be uniformly processed digitally. They are not added as they are spread over a large group of borrowers and thus will be insignificant. Fixed costs will be minimal due to the existing infrastructure of banks and mobile/branchless banking proposed in the model. Profit will depend on the number of accounts and loans advanced by the Sabka Sath wing. If the bank adopts all the principles of the model, the amounts of loans and deposits will rise and lead to a manifold rise in interest income. Table 8.2 summarizes this rather simplistic estimation.

To summarize, the revenue as well as expenditure model of the BoP segment of Sabka Sath wing is commercially viable because:

Table 8.2 Profit and loss account of regular segment and BoP segment of a bank

Existing commercial bank				*Sabka Sath Wing of ANY Bank*			
Revenue Existing banks' average (%)		*Expenditure Entries Existing banks average (%)*		*Revenue (%)*		*Expenditure (%)*	
Interest income from loans and advances	87	Interest paid on deposits	66	Interest income from loans and advances	92	Interest paid on deposits	80
Income from fees, exchange, commissions, etc.	5	Interest on borrowings from RBI and banks	5	Other income (fees, exchange and commissions, etc.)	8	Interest on borrowings from RBI and banks	5
Miscellaneous income, revaluation investments, sale of fixed assets, investments, etc.	8	Staff costs	16	–	–	Staff costs	10
		Other operating expenses	13	–	–	Other operating expenses	5

Source Indicative illustration by authors

1. The cost of capital for Sabka Sath will be less than of the MFIs as having access to the deposit funds; it would not be borrowing much from the banks. Even if it pays interest on deposits, it will be lower than the rate at which MFIs have to borrow.
2. As a result of lower cost of capital, the lending rate for Sabka Sath wing customers can be lower than of the MFIs and the regular borrowers. As per the current estimates, it can be approximately 14–15% lower.
3. The Sabka Sath deposit rate can be 6% which is higher than the maximum rate of 3–4% offered by banks on saving deposits in the regular segment.
4. The operating costs are less due to advanced technology.

On the costs side, staff costs are lower because of the entirely novel administrative infrastructure model. Operating costs are low because of the use of advanced technology. This is feasible in modern times since before computerization and technology use, the staff costs accounted for approximately 65–70% of debits to profit and loss A/c. This meant that transaction costs of manual work were high. Naturally, banks found it difficult to deal with work which involved high volumes of manual handling which gave leeway to MFIs and NGOs. But with the introduction of mobile banking, a radical change has taken place. Banks that had to accept a cost of Rs. 7/- to Rs. 9/- per transaction find that it will cost them less than a rupee.

The *Sabka Sath* model is hypothetical for a prototypical bank. The assumption is that the regulatory infrastructure will be available to support it. In case banks find it difficult to implement the suggested model, they could continue with the earlier arrangement of working through the MFIs and gradually move to that area themselves when they are prepared. The financial part of the model can be further worked out with more details at specific bank level. We lay emphasis on the activity being initiated, if it is not already done.

The model is developed by only taking into consideration the BoP segment of the bank and ignoring the existing business segments. At a later stage, once the new business model delivers, a bank can consider full-fledged diversification into the BoP segment.

Risk Management of the BoP Portfolio

The risk generated through lending to the *Bulk of the Population* customer may be tackled through the state-of-the-art technology.

- Most of the transactions will be cashless. So the risk of frauds may be minimized as compared with the current system.
- The risk of default is a key concern of banks in the case of thin filed customers. Default risk is an indispensable element of lending to any segment.
- Risk is handled by MFIs more or less successfully by close engagement with the borrowers and by monitoring credit history. A combination of appointing localized agents and biometric data bases

collecting and documenting details of borrowers are expected to deal with the default risk.

- Banks should not be overly concerned about the default as the records of lending by MFIs show that the default rates are not high as to make the model unsustainable.
- The model rests on the use of technology and young motivated staff to contain costs and increase outreach.
- MFIs earn and maintain financial viability. Banks can assure a customer that other things remaining the same, when a borrower enquires about a second or third round of loans, they are there to provide it. The ultimate aim of this model is to enable banks to ensure that the borrowers refrain from going to moneylenders whose rates are exploitative.
- The use of cost reducing technology is a key element for the success of the proposed model. India is a global supplier of the Fintech and mobile banking intelligence. However, acceptance of advanced technology by banks can be a limitation in the near future. Fear of the new technology is the topmost concern in today's world. According to *The Banana Skins Report, 2018* (Patel & Lascelles, 2018), the speed with which it is entering the financial markets is perceived as risky by the institutions in the financial inclusion arena (p. 6).

The regulatory framework plays the most important role in reassuring the users and facilitating the use of technology in banking. The financial inclusion landscape consists of various participants like government, the regulator (RBI), banks, SHGs, NGOs, NBFCs, MFIs and SMEs. For achieving complete financial inclusion and alleviation of poverty, these constituents must work in co-ordination. The regulator and the government should nurture customer confidence through efficient regulatory framework and support financial institutions to restructure business models for profitable inclusive growth without hampering their autonomy. Providing access to finance generates positive externalities in terms of poverty reduction. Eventually, social benefit will exceed the private cost of microlending.

Reimagining Inclusive Banking

The book conceptualizes a model for providing a roadmap for the bank business for inclusive banking. The '*Bulk of the Population*' (BoP) has a large collective spending power. Banks need to be convinced of the financial viability of this opportunity offered by the unbanked segment of the BoP. The adoption of this new business model rests on the assumption that regulatory framework supports its application by a bank and also provides regulatory infrastructure for the use of appropriate technology.

On the supply side, lending to the poor by formal institutions fails because of two reasons. Firstly, the poor lack assets to offer as a collateral, and secondly, the costs of credit monitoring are unaffordable. We argue that the second constraint can be removed by banks with the use of advanced technology and newly conceived operational model. Gradually as financial inclusion succeeds, it will reduce poverty and the first constraint will also disappear.

As Rajan puts it, 'Perhaps the most important is the economic condition of the excluded. World over, the poor, the small, and the remote are excluded. It is not just because the financial system is underdeveloped, but because they are hard to service profitably. Nevertheless, this is not a reason to abandon hope, but to ask how we can overcome the impediments in the way of inclusion. The best way to characterize the impediments are through the acronym IIT: Information, Incentives, and Transaction Costs' (Rajan, 2017).

On the demand side, it is crucial for banks to realize that if the customers find the products complex, they will feel uncomfortable and not embrace them. They will feel that they lack an agency for decision-making about their money. In the field surveys conducted by the authors in urban or rural low-income communities in Pune, Nashik and Gulbarga, the respondents stated that they thought that the bank products were complicated and expensive. The survey of SHG members in various parts of the country by the authors revealed that the respondents found bank visits time-consuming and inconvenient as they lost their working day and wages. They were uncomfortable with the documentation in unintelligible jargon. SHG members had hardly any connection with banks. Similar observations were reported by earlier studies.

All these conventional obstacles like screening and monitoring loans and demand side gaps will be removed with the use of technology, and streamlining the administrative structure. But, this can be achieved only if banks change their approach and make an effort to understand the needs, frustrations and aspirations of the low-income segment as they do with their high-income clientele. They should realize that this is their client base in the long term and remain with them for a long time. It will not only benefit the unbanked and underprivileged segment of the population, but also benefit banks themselves to survive in the fiercely competitive environment of systemic distrust. The model envisages that banks embrace the 'bulk of the population' in the low-income segment as their core business clientele, devising products and strategies to attract them. Through the proposed model the authors visualize annihilation of the great divide between 'us' and 'them' through inclusive banking.

Annexure

Three Case Studies of Banks with Successful Implementation of Microlending–Microdeposit Model

1. **Canara Bank, India**

   Canara Bank is successfully implementing financial inclusion, and it received the Skoch Award in Order-of-Merit Category. It took up the implementation of the financial inclusion plan and has a great opportunity to garner the untapped rural potential. According to the Skotch report,[3] 'for the bank, FI is no more a social banking, it is a huge business opportunity'. In 2014 when it received the award, it provided Basic Savings Deposit Accounts to 54.55 lakh people and 142.89 lakh persons since the beginning of the scheme.
2. **Capitec,[4] South Africa**

   In March 2001, its business model included the financially excluded population in banking and maintains the profitability. It has designed specialized products and has a large number of customers satisfied with its customer engagement, low cost fast transactions and helpful staff. It has enabled illiterate rural and financially weaker sections through local access points and use of telecom banking. This case highlights how banks need to start looking at inclusive markets as a growth opportunity rather than a cost to business as they can build a **profitable business** serving a large market of about 500 million people in India.

[3] https://www.skoch.in/images/40summit/casestudy/Canara%20Bank,%20Strategy.pdf.

[4] This case is sourced from Schutte et al. (2013) Designing A Framework To Design A Business Model For The 'Bottom Of The Pyramid' Population, *South African Journal of Industrial Engineering*.

3. **Standard Bank, South Africa**

   Standard Bank Group has provided banking to the low-income groups. This expansion has been undertaken as a response to increasing competition in the banking sector in South Africa. It has adopted the strategy of mobile banking products, high end technology to reduce costs and partnerships across the sector to benefit from linkages and economies of scale. Through access points and branchless banking along with locally appointed community agents, it has succeeded in enhancing financial inclusion of the poor while at the same time retaining its financial profitability.

References

Ayadi, R., & De Groen, W. (2014). *Banking business models monitor 2014: Europe*.

Drucker, P. F. (2017). *The theory of the business (Harvard Business Review Classics)*. Harvard Business Press.

Fredericks, S. P. K. (2015). *Funding for arts and culture in the New South Africa*.

Gamra, S. B., & Plihon, D. (2011). Revenue diversification in emerging market banks: Implications for financial performance. *arXiv preprint arXiv:1107.0170*. https://timesofindia.indiatimes.com/business/india-business/at-rs-6l-cr-banks-fresh-fds-in-q1-double-from-last-year-Updated: Aug 3, 2020, 12:46 IST.

Mauborgne, R., & Kim. (2005). *Blue ocean strategy: How to create uncontested market space and make the competition irrelevant*. Harvard Business School Press.

MFIN Report Q4. (2020, Jan. Mar.). *Microfinance institutions network*. https://mfinindia.org/assets/upload_image/news/pdf/Press%20Release%20-%20Q4%202019-20%20Micrometer.pdf.

Osterwalder, A., & Pigneur, Y. (2010). *Business model generation: A handbook for visionaries, game changers, and challengers*. John Wiley & Sons.

Patel, K., Lascelles, D. (2018). *Finance for All: Wedded to Fintech for Better or Worse*, A CSFI 'Banana Skins' survey of the risks in financial inclusion, Centre for the Study of Financial Innovation (CFSI), CITI, Centre for Financial Inclusion, Accion.

Prahalad, C. K. (2005). *The fortune at the bottom of the pyramid*. Wharton School.

Prahalad, C. K., & Hart, S. L. (2002). The fortune at the bottom of the pyramid. *Strategy + Business*, *26*(2002), 54–67.

Rajan, R. (2017). *I do what i do*. Harper Collins.

RBI Financial Stability Report. (2019, June). https://rbidocs.rbi.org.in/rdocs/PublicationReport/Pdfs/06FSRCHAPTER24945D69340154F559C8A68A24FE5377E.PDF.

Saal, M. et al. (2017, August). Digital financial services: Challenges and opportunities for emerging markets banks. *EM compass note No. 42, International finance corporation.*

Thygesen, N. C., McCauley, R. N., Ma, G., White, W. R., de Haan, J., van den End, W., ... & Balling, M. (2013). 50 years of money and finance: Lessons and challenges. *SUERF 50th anniversary volume-50 years of money and finance: Lessons and challenges.*

Themaat, V. L., Schutte, C. S., Lutters, D., & Kennon, D. (2013). Designing a framework to design a business model for the 'bottom of the pyramid' population. *South African Journal of Industrial Engineering, 24*(3), 190–204.

Index

L. Kulkarni and V. C. Joshi, *Inclusive Banking In India*,
https://doi.org/10.1007/978-981-33-6797-5

The manufacturer's authorised representative in the EU is Springer Nature Customer Service Centre GmbH, Europaplatz 3, 69115 Heidelberg, Germany. If you have any concerns regarding our products, please contact ProductSafety@springernature.com

Printed and bound by CPI Group (UK) Ltd, Croydon, CR0 4YY
30/09/2026
02225455-0002